TEN BATTLES

EVERY CATHOLIC
SHOULD KNOW

TEN BATTLES

EVERY CATHOLIC
SHOULD KNOW

MICHAEL D. GREANEY

TAN Books
Charlotte, North Carolina

Cover design by Caroline Green

Cover image: Polish Husaria © Mariusz Józef Kozik, Poland

Library of Congress Control Number: 2017954994

ISBN: 978-1-5051-1020-3

Published in the United States by
TAN Books
P.O. Box 269
Gastonia NC 28053
www.TANBooks.com

Printed and bound in India

To my mother, who waited, but did not live to see it

CONTENTS

vii

PUBLISHER'S INTRODUCTION

As George Santayana said, "Those who cannot remember the past are condemned to repeat it." Few these days, however, even learn enough of the past to remember anything in the first place; cultural illiteracy is almost universal in the West. Consequently, many people are stuck in what Santayana called the "perpetual infancy" of failing to know either where they came from or where they are going.

Much of the blame for this can be placed squarely on academia, which long ago drifted away from education into job training, and has now degenerated from job training into babysitting. Safe spaces take the place of discussions and debates, while new ideas are rejected as microaggressions forced on others with trigger words, a statue, or even a funny look or two.

America's culture shows the results of academia's failure. In the summer of 2017, for example, an article appeared chronicling the declining interest in history, "Americans' Declining Interest In History Is Hitting Museums Like Colonial Williamsburg Hard."[1]

The statistics, even if they are considered worse than lies or damned lies, are depressing. They tell us that Americans

---

[1]   Jennifer Tiedemann and Karen Marsico, "Americans' Declining Interest In History Is Hitting Museums Like Colonial Williamsburg Hard," *The Federalist*, http://www.thefederalist.com/2017/08/22/americans-declining-interest-history-hitting-colonial-williamsburg-hard-not-one, accessed August 24, 2017.

do not visit historical sites in their own country with any frequency, and that number has been in continual decline for decades. Between 1982 and 2012, for example, attendance by people over eighteen went down 13 percent overall; the figure is worse for those eighteen to twenty-four years of age. The number of students taking history classes at colleges and universities fell by nearly 8 percent from 2012 to 2015, while the number of history majors dropped 12 percent over the same period.

No doubt a large part of the problem is that what passes for history these days bears very little resemblance to what actually happened. Nor does it fit into any perspective other than a vague liberal agenda and the cause du jour.

Students are saddled with politically correct "interpretations" and "viewpoints" regarding how they are supposed to think about something instead of just being told the story and allowed to form their own opinions from the evidence. As a result, students know what attitudes and opinions they need in order to achieve popularity or acceptability in modern society—or simply to avoid finding themselves on the wrong end of a club wielded by some Antifa thug—but often have no idea why they think the way they end up thinking . . . if they think at all.

That, however, is not education, but indoctrination and brainwashing. As Saint Augustine of Hippo pointed out:

> Do teachers ever claim that it is their own thoughts that are grasped and retained, rather than the branches of learning themselves that they purport to transmit by their speaking? What foolish curiosity could ever prompt a man to send his child to school in order to have him learn what the teacher thinks? When teachers have made use of words to explain all those branches of learning, however . . . then those who are . . .

pupils reflect within themselves whether what has been said is true—contemplating, that is, that inner truth according to their capacity. It is then, therefore, that they learn.[2]

It comes as no surprise, then, that so few people are interested in history these days, for the story has been lost in favor of forcing correct opinions onto students. Again, at the risk of repeating ourselves, many westerners today have no idea where they came from and even less of an idea where they are heading.

If that is true of our own history, matters are even worse once we venture beyond our own culture. To most Americans and, to a lesser extent, western Europeans, the story of central and eastern Europe, as well as Asia Minor, is completely unknown territory, a sort of tabula rasa or blank spot on the map.

That fact is most unfortunate, for the history of those areas has had a profound effect on the history of the world. The region was the center of civilization for thousands of years, at a time when western Europe was considered the edge of the world and the Americas were virtually unknown, except for rumors dismissed by most people as mere fables.

That is why this book should be of interest far beyond its obvious target audience of Catholics Who Want to Know About Famous Battles. Particularly in recent years, eastern Europe and Asia Minor have been in the news, but few people realize just how far back the region has been making news—or why.

---

[2]   Saint Augustine, *De Magistro*, § 45.

To say that today's global situation is the result of the post-Cold War "clash of civilizations" is—while correct up to a point—to give a description rather than a reason and to merely assert rather than tell a story. The aim of this book is to tell the story of the struggle between the Ottoman Turks and the forces of Christendom. Covering the centuries-long war against militant Islam—as personified by the Grand Turk—from the Dreadful Day of Manzikert in 1071, climaxing in the battle of Lepanto in 1571 half a millennium later, to the beginning of the final decline with the siege of Khotim in 1622, *Ten Battles Every Catholic Should Know* presents key battles that marked turning points. Less well known than the struggle to retake Spain and Southern France, the battlefields of Armenia and eastern and central Europe were just as crucial to preserve Christendom.

There is the battle of Manzikert, which marked the beginning of the fight, and the real Dracula, Vlad III of Wallachia, who carried out a personal crusade against the Turks to such good effect that his name strikes terror down to the present day. The battle of Mohács, "the Tomb of Hungary," is related, as is the siege of Vienna in 1529, the first setback experienced by Süleymân the Magnificent, perhaps the greatest ruler the Ottoman Turks ever knew.

Perhaps of greatest interest is the buildup to the climactic Great Siege of Malta and the battle of Lepanto; the siege of Szigetvár (the "Hungarian Alamo"), and those of Nicosia and Famagusta on the island of Cyprus, the heroism of which inspired the soldiers and sailors at Lepanto. The accounts of battles are enlivened and expanded with historical footnotes and introductions explaining important and interesting details.

What results is a stirring, popular, but richly detailed, account of an often-overlooked period in history that nevertheless presents a more objective viewpoint than others in the field. Our title is perhaps not ambitious enough, for truly these are ten battles that should be known not just by every Catholic but by every individual with even a passing interest in history or current events. For this is a story that continues to unfold today.

1

MANZIKERT

1071

*B*YZANTINE is exactly the right word to describe the politics of the Eastern Roman Empire in the latter half of the eleventh century. Due to an ongoing power grab by the bureaucratic *élite* of the empire since the days of Basil II, fifty years before, the army was in deplorable shape. Morale was low, and relatively few soldiers were Roman citizens[3] under the direct control of their commander-in-chief.

The small landholding peasants, the backbone of the imperial army for over fifteen hundred years, had gradually been dispossessed of their capital in favor of the old aristocrats and new industrialists. Because many citizens, subsisting on wages and lacking ownership income, could no longer afford the expensive equipment required to be soldiers, and because the relatively few small owners among them tended to be personally loyal to the basileus instead of to a faceless bureaucracy, there had been an explicit move toward the use of mercenaries.

The idea was that using mercenaries would decrease the power of the military by making a military coup less likely.

---

[3]   Byzantines referred to themselves as Romans, even though they spoke Greek and their capital was Constantinople.

1

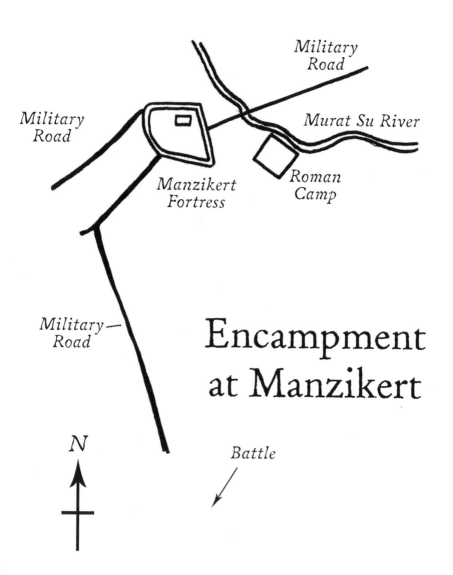

Military
Road

Military
Road

Murat Su River

Manzikert
Fortress

Roman
Camp

Military
Road

Encampment
at Manzikert

N

Battle

It would also, at the same time, increase the power of the bureaucratic party. The latest attempt to reverse this policy was the ascension of Romanus IV Diogenes. Still, as the bureaucratic *élite* grew in power, that of the military decreased in proportion.

Romanus Diogenes's predecessor, Constantine X Ducas, was a scholar who preferred to spend hours splitting hairs on legal matters instead of paying attention to national security. He was also a creature of the great (and treacherous) scholar Michael Psellus, who sought to be the power behind the throne—which he could only do when the bureaucracy, not the military, was in the ascendant.

Although Constantine came from the military aristocracy, he feared and despised the military. An outstanding orator like his teacher Psellus, he was able to sway people to his point of view even when they knew it was against the best interests of the state.

Even with the arrival on the scene of a new threat in the form of the Seljuk Turks, Constantine's every move was designed to weaken the military and strengthen the bureaucracy. As he was dying, he made his soon-to-be widow, Eudocia, swear an oath not to remarry and exacted written promises from key members of the court that they would only recognize a member of his immediate family as head of state. This would prevent anyone from becoming basileus—usually mistranslated as "emperor"—in Eudocia's right by marrying her.

After Constantine's death, fully aware that the empire needed a radical overhaul and a strong military if it was to survive, Eudocia spread the rumor that she desired marriage with the dissolute brother of the Patriarch John Xiphilinus.

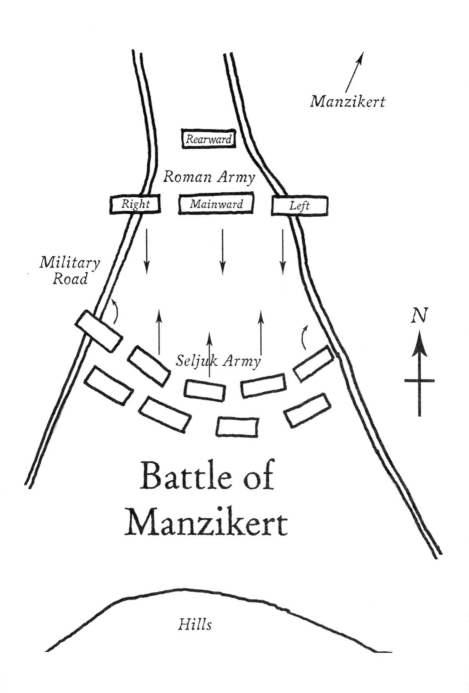

Manzikert

Rearward

Roman Army

Right   Mainward   Left

Military
Road

Seljuk Army

N

Battle of
Manzikert

Hills

The patriarch's brother was a notorious womanizer, but one whom Xiphilinus and his good friend Michael Psellus could easily control.

Xiphilinus, of course, was delighted. A dispensation from Eudocia's oath not to remarry, however, required the consent of not only the patriarch but the Senate as well. The dispensation was soon forthcoming. Eudocia, however, then announced her betrothal not to the patriarch's brother but to the bureaucratic party's worst nightmare. This was Romanus Diogenes, who married Eudocia and assumed the throne in 1068.

The new basileus was arrogant and had a high opinion of himself, although unlike many such cases it was in some measure justified. He was a hardworking and able administrator as well as a skilled military commander.

Romanus Diogenes also had a strong sense of duty and had defied—and been accused of trying to overthrow—Constantine X when it was obvious the latter's policies were laying the groundwork for disaster. He had been exiled (suggesting that accusations of planning a coup were specious), the ban being lifted only on Constantine's death.

Unfortunately, the new basileus had too little time to repair the damage done by half a century of bureaucratic incompetence and hostility against the military. . . .

THE DREADFUL DAY

Romanus IV Diogenes, Basileus of the Romans, in a twist on the advice of Ozymandius, might have been tempted to look on his own works and despair. Throughout the long, hot, and dusty day in late August of 1071 on the steppe near the Armenian fortress of Manzikert, he had struggled to come to grips with the enemy but had become increasingly frustrated. Over the course of the afternoon, the imperial army had advanced across the steppe. There had been no real engagement since the day before. The Seljuk army had withdrawn as the Romans came forward. The enemy had formed a wide crescent that might have put Romanus Diogenes uneasily in mind of the Greek lines at Marathon, fifteen centuries before.

Nevertheless, the Roman army was not as yet in real peril. Mounted archers had harassed the troops every step of the way, galloping up and down the ranks of the Romans and letting loose a continual rain of arrows. This was similar to tactics employed in the American west by native peoples and throughout history whenever light cavalry faced a less mobile foe.

The result was everything that the enemy could hope for. The imperial cataphracti—precursors of the medieval knight—would break ranks and go charging after the Seljuk skirmishers.

This was probably against orders. An experienced commander, Romanus Diogenes would have known better than most the danger of letting troops, even the magnificent imperial heavy cavalry, go off on their own initiative, abandoning their place in line.

The basileus, however, had not been able to stop them. He had been losing control of the situation for the past three days, and probably well before that.

The reason is not difficult to discern. When Romanus Diogenes set out on his expedition, the bulk of his army was made up of conscripts, foreign mercenaries paid by the bureaucracy, and levies of bucellarii—household troops—under the direct command of their private employers.

A bucellarius was a mercenary soldier hired by the nobility or anyone else with sufficient wealth to maintain a private army. Bucellarii were often (as might be expected) arrogant, ill equipped to follow the orders of anyone except their own immediate commanders, and supremely self-assured.

Under a wise and patriotic commander, such as the famous Count Belisarius in the time of Justinian the Great, bucellarii could provide a useful, non-political addition to the military. In the pay of and under a genius like Belisarius who had the good of the state at heart, they could even effectively supplant the military, which was always a prime target for special interests in the Roman Empire—East or West.

Unfortunately, the current commander of the bucellarii, Andronicus Ducas, nephew of Constantine X Ducas, was the perfect choice for his current position; that is, Andronicus Ducas was the perfect choice if the goal was to destroy the effectiveness of imperial forces.

Andronicus Ducas had a positive genius for encouraging all the bad qualities of the bucellarii and did nothing to enhance what virtues they may have possessed. In addition, he harbored a grudge against Romanus Diogenes.

Andronicus Ducas felt that his father, John Ducas Caesar, brother of Constantine X Ducas, had been denied his rightful place as basileus. This, of course, displaced Andronicus Ducas as heir-apparent.

Probably fully aware of the animosity of Andronicus Ducas and the unreliability of the nobility and their household troops, Romanus Diogenes assigned them to the rearguard or rearward. Normally this would have kept them almost completely out of action except in the event of a complete disaster or when pursuing a defeated enemy. Under such circumstances, any misplaced initiative could cause little harm. In view of the charge-and-retreat tactics adopted by the Seljuk invasion force, however, the incompetence of Andronicus Ducas, intrinsic or assumed, was given full play.

The imperial cavalry, the bulk of them Roman only by courtesy and contract, pursued the enemy into the foothills, where they were caught in carefully prepared ambushes. They should have learned their lesson after the first such incident, but discipline had broken down almost completely by this time. Emotion ruled the ranks instead of reason and training.

Now the sun was beginning to go down on a day that, so far, had been at least as bad as the preceding week. That, too, had been remarkably frustrating.

It had begun well, however. Five days previously, the fortress of Manzikert, south of the Euphrates and north of Lake Van, had fallen into Romanus Diogenes's hands like a ripe plum. There had been no fight. The basileus had been able to reoccupy the fortress, deep in the strategic province of Armenia, with ease. The Seljuks had taken the fortress only a few years before.

It was not until later that Romanus Diogenes received word that Strategos Joseph Tarchaniotes had been soundly defeated. Tarchaniotes was in command of the greater part of the imperial army.

Tarchaniotes and his troops had been detached to take and hold Khelat, a Seljuk-held strongpoint some *stadia*[4] to the south of Manzikert near the shores of Lake Van. So soundly had he been routed, in fact, that Romanus Diogenes probably suspected treason. Tarchaniotes was a known intimate of Andronicus Ducas and a strong supporter of the bureaucratic party that had opposed the ascension of Romanus Diogenes.

Tarchaniotes's sudden and incomprehensible retreat may have been inspired more by a desire for political revenge than any genuine military reversal. As is typical with the shortsighted bureaucratic mindset, the *strategos*—the word can be understood as "general"—may truly not have realized the implications of a military setback at this time or may have placed personal political motives above love of country.

According to the few reports that survive, Strategos Tarchaniotes had barely engaged the enemy when his forty thousand men, who happened to outnumber the Seljuks facing them, went into headlong flight. A few hundred of the more loyal troops appear to have made their way to Manzikert after the precipitous retreat.

These rejoined the smaller part of the army encamped at the fortress with the basileus. The bulk of them, however, followed Tarchaniotes and ran a race all the way to Melitene, a town on the Euphrates. The Seljuks evidently

---

[4] A *stadium* (pl. *stadia*) is the equivalent of a furlong, or an eighth of a mile.

did not think it worthwhile to pursue, which may constitute additional evidence that the defeat had been prearranged.

At a single stroke, and without inflicting any damage on the enemy, Romanus Diogenes had lost more than half his army. He is estimated to have had no more than thirty or forty thousand men remaining of the eighty thousand with which he began the campaign.

Early the next day, Romanus Diogenes sent out detachments to forage. They were set upon by Seljuk bowmen and suffered heavy casualties.

Probably under the impression that he was dealing with nothing more than some stray bands of enemy horsemen, Romanus Diogenes sent out a small detachment under Strategos Nicephorus Bryennius to reinforce the foraging expedition. Bryennius was a reliable man, and considered loyal to Romanus Diogenes and the military party.

Romanus Diogenes was unable to believe his ears when Bryennius returned, barely an hour and a half later. He did not bring news of a victory, but a demand for reinforcements. His increasingly frayed nerves caused Romanus Diogenes to explode in a shockingly uncharacteristic temper tantrum.

This display of temper appears to have been building up through the whole campaign. It indicates that the basileus knew something was amiss from the very beginning.

A few hundred stadia out of Constantinople, Romanus Diogenes had begun to exhibit an odd remoteness, ill temper, impatience with advice, and a most atypical streak of cruelty. At one point in the campaign, a Roman soldier was accused of stealing an ass from a local peasant. He was brought before Romanus Diogenes and sentenced to the outdated punishment of having his nose cut off.

An eyewitness to this seemingly trivial incident was Michael Attaleiates, a strategos who left the best surviving account of the battle. He stated that he himself began to entertain suspicions of impending disaster when Romanus Diogenes insisted on the sentence being carried out even after the soldier had appealed to the intercession of the icon of the Holy Virgin of Blachernae.

The holy icon was always carried by the basileus into battle and was thought to ensure victory. This, of course, could be nothing more than the usual 20/20 hindsight so common in these situations, but the fact that the incident stuck in Attaleiates's mind is probably indicative of the unusual nature of Romanus Diogenes's behavior.

There were other incidents.

Romanus Diogenes had begun setting up his own camp, apart from the established bivouac. Later, he ordered that his private possessions be separated from those of the rest of the army.

There were reports that the basileus had been disturbed by bad omens. These included the central pole of his tent breaking suddenly and an unexplained fire that destroyed much of his personal equipment as well as killing some of his best horses and mules.

Still, none of this excused Romanus Diogenes's conduct toward Necephorus Bryennius. Clearly the man had run into something more than a mere band of marauders. It began to sound as if he had encountered the entire vanguard of the Seljuk army.

After trying to figure out the best course to take, Romanus Diogenes sent out a relief party under Strategos Basilacius, an Armenian known for his impetuous action. It seemed to be exactly what the situation called for. The Armenian, at least, would not be tempted to turn tail and run like Tarchaniotes. Besides, the other generals whom Romanus Diogenes could trust were probably needed in camp to keep an eye on those whom he could not.

It proved to be a disastrous decision. Basilacius attempted to pursue the enemy horsemen but was trapped in an ambush and surrounded. The Seljuk soldiers rode circles around the Romans, shooting arrows constantly into the massed group. A few of the soldiers managed to escape, but Strategos Basilacius, for once his impulsiveness playing him false, was captured.

This time acting decisively, Romanus Diogenes quickly sent out Bryennius again with orders to rescue the rescuers. He was accompanied not with a small force this time but with a substantial number of soldiers.

Unfortunately, Bryennius came up against more than just the vanguard of the Seljuk army. The vanguard by itself could have been handled, even with the Roman force considerably weakened by the desertion of the troops under Tarchaniotes. Instead, it appeared that nearly the whole of the Seljuk army had turned out, possibly three-quarters of their entire strength.

Bryennius was completely outnumbered. Keeping his head, the strategos ordered a retreat, and his men retired in good order back to the camp around Manzikert.

The general himself, however, was wounded three times—twice in the back from arrows and once in the front from a lance. The wounds proved to be superficial, and Bryennius was up and about the next day.

The following night had been completely moonless, and the Roman army had gotten as little sleep as there was light. Seljuk skirmishers charged time and again at the palisade surrounding the camp, coming just close enough to loose volleys of arrows and then retreating out of range. In addition, they kept up a constant barrage of noise, inflicting almost more damage, at least to morale, than they did with the arrows by depriving the Roman soldiers of necessary sleep.

On several occasions rumors spread through the ranks that the defenses had been breached and the camp was being overrun, but these proved to be groundless. The rumors did, however, greatly assist the enemy in their efforts to keep the Romans awake and sleepless.

Everyone was delighted the next morning when it was discovered that the defenses had held after all. This, however, was soon overshadowed by the news that a large contingent of Uz mercenaries had deserted during the night to the Seljuks.

The Uz were of the same ethnic makeup as a large proportion of the enemy army and probably found a ready welcome in the ranks. Romanus Diogenes had several other related groups in his army, any one or all of which might suddenly take it into their heads to desert as well. More troops had to be detached to keep an eye on them.

Over half of Romanus Diogenes's army had by now simply evaporated on the eve of an important battle with nothing gained in the process. Most of those who remained, he had good reason to consider unreliable.

Romanus Diogenes then sat tight for two days while he reorganized what remained of his troops. In the face of desertions and outright treason, he had to be very careful about which troops he trusted and where he positioned them. At that point, a Seljuk delegation arrived with the offer of a truce. Ostensibly from the caliph in Baghdad, it was more likely a personal initiative of Alp Arslan, the Seljuk commander and "Sultan of Rum," or "Sultan of the Roman Lands," a slightly anticipatory title which proved to be more than a little prescient.

This move probably surprised Romanus Diogenes far more than the military defeats already inflicted on his army. It was not just the offer of a truce from an enemy who had yet to make a single mistake or lose even a minor engagement, other than surrendering Manzikert without a fight. Even that could be construed as a strategic withdrawal rather than a defeat.

Romanus Diogenes now faced the most serious military decision of his career. He was expecting momentarily to be overwhelmed, yet here was the enemy commander requesting a truce. The only possible answer was that it was a trick.

Apparently, the enemy commander thought that further delay, such as one engendered by a truce, would only weaken the Roman army. He was absolutely right. Any more desertions would so reduce Romanus Diogenes's force that he would have little hope of even retreating in good order. It was also possible that something had happened in the enemy army that required some time to repair, just as Romanus Diogenes had been hard pressed to reorganize his entire force in the face of the enemy.

In either case, Romanus Diogenes probably felt that his only option was to attack immediately, while he still had a sufficient number of effectives to carry it off. He may have felt that the request for a truce might be a signal that the enemy was weak enough to be overcome, even by a reduced and demoralized Roman force. Consequently, the following day, August 26, 1071, Romanus Diogenes, Basileus of the Romans, ordered an attack.

He was now paying for that decision. All day, he had been unable to engage the enemy. Now, with the sun beginning to set, he was rapidly losing the opportunity to do anything except withdraw. He ordered the imperial standards reversed and turned his horse around.

This was a fatal decision.

The large number of mercenaries in the Roman army had not been properly trained. Not realizing that the reversal of the imperial standards was the usual signal for a withdrawal, the majority interpreted it as a surrender or a sign that the basileus had been killed.

The fact that many of the regulars did understand the signal only meant that things were even more confused. The Roman formations wavered and then broke apart.

This gave the Seljuks the chance for which they had been waiting all day. Observing the massive confusion, they charged through the now disordered ranks.

The Seljuks wheeled behind the main body of troops and separated it from the rearguard. This placed them in a dangerously exposed position, but Arp Arslan may have felt that the risk was worth the gain.

His hunch turned out to be exactly right. There is also the possibility that, through treachery in the Roman ranks, he was acting on certain knowledge of the response to such a move.

This was because the rearguard was still under the command of Andronicus Ducas. Instead of advancing and catching the Seljuks between the two lines, Andronicus Ducas seems to have decided it was time to complete the work begun by his compatriot Joseph Tarchaniotes. He declared that the basileus had been defeated, and the battle was lost.

The entire rearguard turned and fled. They were followed by more and more contingents of the center and the right wing of the mainward (the main body or "battle" of troops) as the army saw its last hope disappear in a display of either arrant cowardice or outright treason.

Only the left wing of the mainward now remained intact. In the deepening twilight, they advanced and attempted to rescue Romanus Diogenes. The Seljuks managed to get behind them, too, and attack.

The Seljuks were thereby able to draw the left wing off until the only effective imperial force on the field was forced to retreat. The remnants of the once-proud Roman army made its way back to the camp around Manzikert in a panic.

It was of no avail. Utter chaos reigned everywhere. Some rumors maintained that the basileus was still fighting with what remained of the army, others that he had been killed or captured. Everyone had a different opinion, and everyone gave it in as loud a voice as possible.

The Seljuks kept up the pressure, carrying out their famous tactic of encircling the scattered groups of Romans and shooting a constant barrage of arrows. Some were killed, others captured, while still others were simply run down and trampled beneath the hooves of the enemy horse. In the words of a surviving eyewitness, it seemed as though the whole Roman state was overturned and the empire itself was on the verge of collapse.

Meanwhile, surrounded by his personal guard, Romanus Diogenes stood his ground and fought. He had called on his troops to rally but, in the noise and confusion, had either been unheard or ignored.

It seemed that the only safety lay in flight, but a Roman basileus does not run from an enemy. He either kills or is killed. There was no alternative for a Roman. Romanus Diogenes fought on.

Had he been other than the man he was, Romanus Diogenes could probably have made good his escape. His Armenian conscripts, believing it made no difference to them whether the hated Byzantines or the unknown Seljuks ruled them, had been among the first to desert. The mercenaries, too, forsook their contract and absconded with their money secured.

The Armenians and the mercenaries could almost be forgiven, however. For either group, abandoning the fight smacked more of long-sighted prudence than cowardice or shortsighted treason.

The real treachery was the flight of the bucellarii, the private armies of the nobles of the bureaucratic party that manned the rearguard under their commander, Andronicus Ducas. Even if it were due to cowardice—which it probably was not—the job of the rearguard is to act as a reserve to pursue a defeated enemy, prevent the main force from being flanked, and to cover a retreat. In the event a battle line starts to dissolve, the rearguard is moved up to stiffen the ranks and restore order.

In order to carry out its mission, the rearguard generally occupies the most secure position. In this case, it also made it easy for Andronicus Ducas and his soldiers to turn tail and run while incurring little or no danger to themselves.

Still Romanus Diogenes fought on. Even after his horse was killed from under him, he did not surrender until his wounds made it impossible for him to hold his sword.

The next morning, after a night spent among other prisoners, Romanus Diogenes was brought before the sultan in chains. At first, Alp Arslan could not believe that the man before him was the Roman basileus.

The testimony of former Seljuk envoys and that of Romanus Diogenes's fellow prisoner Basilacius finally convinced the sultan that this was, indeed, the Roman commander. Alp Arslan immediately performed the ceremony accepting an enemy's unconditional surrender by ordering Romanus Diogenes to kiss the ground before him and placing his foot on the Roman commander's neck.

That this was a symbolic gesture purely for form's sake was made clear by the fact that the sultan then personally helped Romanus Diogenes to his feet and sat the basileus down beside him at his right hand. By doing so, Alp Arslan raised the Roman commander's status from defeated enemy to honored guest.

From then on, Romanus Diogenes was treated with every possible courtesy. He ate at the sultan's table and received great sympathy from Alp Arslan for the treachery that had put the Roman in his power.

The worst Romanus Diogenes had to bear were a few well-placed comments from the sultan criticizing Byzantine military operations. Even these, although coming from the victor, came across more as helpful advice than condemnation.

While all of this sounds very odd, especially considering the character of later Turkish campaigns, there was a method in the sultan's madness. As a defeated yet mature and able ruler, Romanus Diogenes was much more valuable to him than the unknown quantity a new and untried basileus would be.

Alp Arslan would be able to turn his back on Romanus Diogenes and be reasonably certain he would not be attacked from the rear. This was all-important because the sultan's goal was not Byzantium. He had a long-time ambition to destroy the Fatimid Caliphate in Egypt.

The sultan had, in fact, been preparing to depart on an Egyptian campaign when word reached him of the Byzantine expedition to retake Armenia. Already unable to control the Turkoman raiders that plagued both the Byzantines and the Seljuks, Alp Arslan had felt himself forced to put off the African expedition and deal with the new threat.

These circumstances made the peace negotiations almost cordial. Anxious to start the Egyptian adventure, Alp Arslan gave up all claims to Armenia and demanded only the surrender of the fortress of Manzikert (which he already held) and the cities of Antioch, Edessa, and Hieropolis, along with one of Romanus Diogenes's daughters as a bride for one of his sons. He asked ten million gold solidi as the basileus's ransom.

Equally anxious to return to Constantinople as soon as possible to retain the throne, Romanus Diogenes readily agreed to most of these extraordinarily moderate demands. He pointed out, however, that the imperial treasury did not have ten million solidi to spare after fitting out the expedition that Alp Arslan had just defeated.

Astonishingly, the sultan agreed. The ransom was reduced to 1 million solidi and an annual tribute of 360,000, which was much less expensive than a continued war. He also urged Romanus Diogenes to return to Constantinople at the earliest possible moment, probably as aware as the basileus that potential treachery was not limited to the battlefield, and no one other than Romanus Diogenes could be trusted to keep the treaty.

Consequently, barely a week after the battle, Romanus Diogenes began his return journey with full imperial honors. He was given an escort of two emirs and a hundred mamelukes, members of an elite military group, while Alp Arslan himself rode next to him on the first stage of the journey. Incredibly, Romanus Diogenes had effectively been handed what amounted to a draw in place of a total defeat.

Unfortunately, the bureaucrats in Constantinople did not see it that way. They had not wanted Romanus Diogenes on the throne in the first place, preferring someone they could manipulate.

To complicate matters, a month after Romanus Diogenes had set out on his ill-fated expedition, word had come that the city of Bari, the last Byzantine possession in the Italian peninsula, had fallen to the Normans after a three-year siege. News of the defeat at Manzikert spread confusion through the capital. The only thing everyone could agree on was that Romanus Diogenes—if he lived—had forfeited the throne. The question, however, was who would replace him. Should Eudocia resume power? What about Michael, her oldest son by Constantine X Ducas? Perhaps, as Michael was weak, he and his two younger brothers, Andronicus and Constantine, could rule as a triumvirate? Such an arrangement was not unheard of; once, eight German brothers had shared a crown. As is so often the case in such situations, he who moved first seized power. This was John Ducas Caesar, brother of Constantine X Ducas. Romanus Diogenes had exiled him to Bithynia just before setting out on his ill-fated expedition, and John Ducas had hurried back to Constantinople the moment he heard of the disaster.

Clearly wanting the throne for himself, but backed only by a small faction, John Ducas ostensibly supported the claim of his nephew Michael, whom he could easily control once his mother, Eudocia, was eliminated. He was ably assisted in this effort by his son, Andronicus Ducas, who had just returned, fresh from his betrayal of the basileus at Manzikert.

Although his faction was small, John Ducas had the backing of the famed Varangian Guard. These were Norse mercenaries drawn from Russianized Vikings (from whence they got their name) as well as some from Scandinavia. John Ducas divided the guard into two contingents.

And so one group, under Andronicus Ducas, went through the palace announcing that Michael was the new basileus. The other, under John Ducas, arrested Eudocia, later forcing her to take religious vows and enter a convent. Michael VII Ducas became basileus of the Empire of the Romans.

Suggesting that even sycophantic court chroniclers could have a sense of shame, what happened next is vague. Romanus Diogenes gathered the remnants of his army and seems to have engaged in—and lost—two battles, the second against his erstwhile commander of the rearguard, Andronicus Ducas.

After receiving a holy oath sworn in the presence of three archbishops that he would not be harmed, Romanus Diogenes surrendered to Andronicus Ducas on condition that he renounce all claims to the throne and retire to a monastery. He was immediately seized and, right before the horrified archbishops, blinded and tied to a mule for the long journey to Constantinople.

Romanus Diogenes died in agony a few days after his arrival in the Queen City. It is said, however, that he never once uttered any curse or blasphemy, but instead gave thanks to God and bore whatever happened to him with great courage.

Michael VII Ducas, of course, refused to honor the treaty with Alp Arslan, which gave the Seljuks all the excuse they needed to invade two years later. This time, however, the Byzantines were faced not with the more or less civilized Seljuks, but with tens of thousands of Turkoman savages, whose conversion to Islam seems only to have added religious fanaticism to their almost unbelievable ferocity and cruelty.

Byzantium now went from disaster to disaster. Within a few generations, virtually the whole of the imperial territory was lost. The once mighty Eastern Roman Empire would linger on for another four centuries, but it died at Manzikert.

HISTORICAL NOTE: THE FIRST CRUSADER

A combination of treachery and incompetence defeated Romanus IV Diogenes at the battle of Manzikert. Ironically, both can be traced to the same cause: the economic disenfranchisement of the ordinary citizen through loss of private property and the subsequent growth in the power of a bureaucratic government.

Roman history, Latin or Greek, graphically demonstrates the importance of widespread ownership to national security—and the inevitable tendency of the rich and powerful to concentrate ownership, whether privately (capitalism) or publicly (socialism), to the detriment of national wellbeing, even disaster.

The political as well as economic importance of widespread ownership of the means of production has been recognized from the earliest times. As Plutarch had Tiberius Gracchus declare in a speech in his *Lives of the Noble Grecians and Romans* (the classic John Dryden translation),

> He told them that the commanders were guilty of a ridiculous error, when, at the head of their armies, they exhorted the common soldiers to fight for their sepulchers and altars; when not any amongst so many Romans is possessed of either altar or monument, neither have they any houses of their own, or hearths of their ancestors to defend. They fought indeed and were slain, but it was to maintain the luxury and the wealth of other men. They were styled the masters of the world, but in the meantime had not one foot of ground which they could call their own.

Not surprisingly, it was widespread ownership of landed capital that secured the economic and military might of Byzantium from the seventh to the eleventh centuries. This covered the period from the restoration of the empire by Heraclius to the disaster of Manzikert.

It was in the year 610 that Heraclius, whom Lord John Julius Norwich with a great deal of justice called "the First Crusader," became basileus. All signs pointed to the very real possibility that he would be the last. The empire was dissolving before his eyes.

Greece had been lost to the Slavs, while the Persians were rampaging throughout Asia Minor. Jerusalem had fallen, and the True Cross and other sacred relics of the Crucifixion had been carried off. A number of shrines, including the Church of the Holy Sepulcher, had been pillaged and burned. Chaos reigned.

Instead of rushing headlong into battle and dying with great glory and even greater futility—at which many subsequent historians expressed complete bafflement—Heraclius set about completely reorganizing the imperial government and the economy. Faced with an empty treasury, a demoralized army, and a hopelessly corrupt bureaucracy, his was a daunting task.

Heraclius's first act was to divide the territory remaining to him into "themes," a term previously used for a division of troops. In place of the former complete centralization, power was devolved, with each theme being semi-autonomous under a strategos, who served as both civil governor and military commander.

Large numbers of new villages were established, colonized by soldiers and potential soldiers. These received what amounted to freehold grants of land, subject only to hereditary military service by the landowner or his eldest son whenever demanded. Each received a small stipend, which helped defray the cost of arms, armor, and the horses and mules—essential to campaigning over great distances—which each man was expected to maintain.

At one stroke, Heraclius created a solid national army of native, land-owning, battle-ready reservists who could be called up at any time and who, simultaneously, began a restoration of the tax base. This replaced the haphazard use of conscripts and mercenaries, both notoriously uncertain in number and unreliable in battle as well as untrained in organized warfare.

The economic benefits were not immediately realized, however, and Heraclius still had to raise money for his campaign to drive out the Persians and conquer the Slavs. Increased taxes, forced loans, advances from rich relatives and friends, and heavy fines on corrupt bureaucrats provided some funding.

The primary source of cash, however, came from the Orthodox Church. Somewhat apocalyptically, the Patriarch Sergius considered the war the final conflict between the holy armies of Christ and the fire-worshipping Zoroastrians.

Sergius overlooked certain irregularities in Heraclius's private life and patriotically put the financial resources of the entire Church, from the smallest parish up to the largest monastery and archdiocese, at the disposal of the basileus. Heraclius gratefully accepted.

Finally, after twelve years and a series of adventures that sound like the plot of a bad historical novel, Heraclius was ready. He carefully selected as training ground an area only a few stadia from where Alexander the Great had landed in his campaign against the Persians.

There, the basileus spent the entire summer of 622 engaged in intensive training and morale building. He told his soldiers repeatedly that they were God's chosen instruments against the forces of Antichrist. The Lord of Hosts would himself ensure their victory.

Modern skeptics might be tempted to argue or sneer, but the appeal to faith and patriotism was effective. Heraclius succeeded, although the war that began that autumn was long and difficult.

Heraclius's reforms saved the empire, but even they could be improved. During his reign, despite the reorganization, a few great magnates still controlled most of the land. A century later, as reflected in "the Farmers' Law" of the late seventh or early eighth century, small holdings had proliferated thanks to Heraclius's colonization program, a sort of medieval Homestead Act.

This created a great and growing reserve army for the empire composed of provincial militia whose strength derived from the economic power of widespread capital ownership. This social arrangement maintained the security of the state until the bureaucratic party, envious of the economic independence of the common people and fearful of the military, began undermining both by destroying small ownership and concentrating power in the hands of the government administration that they controlled.

2

WALLACHIA

1462

FOLLOWING the battle of Manzikert, the Turks expanded rapidly into Anatolia. Its territory much reduced, the Byzantine Empire experienced an economic recovery thanks to its key trading position. Constantinople became the largest and wealthiest city in Europe, which made it a tempting target during the Fourth Crusade. The city was sacked, and its remaining territories split between Latin and Greek spheres of influence.

Even after the recovery of Constantinople in 1261, the Byzantine Empire remained only one of a number of small states in the area. These gradually fell to the Turks, with the Queen City herself taken. Constantine XI Palaiologos, the last basileus, died fighting in the final Ottoman assault on May 29, 1453.

Flushed with victory, Sultan Mehmet II went on to conquer Serbia from 1454 to 1459, the Despotate of Morea (an area in the Peloponnese) in 1460, and the Trebizond Empire in northeastern Anatolia (now Turkey) in 1461. It seemed as if the unstoppable Ottoman armies would soon invade the heart of Europe.

Then they met Vlad. . . .

VLAD'S CRUSADE

It was a scene out of hell. Save for the occasional involuntary intake of breath, made difficult by the stench of death, the silence was broken only by the cries of carrion birds that circled, disturbed by the approach of living men. These wheeled and turned, or observed the newcomers with a certain macabre curiosity from their nests in the skulls and ribcages of the dead.

Proceeding slowly, the advance guard of the Ottoman host walked in stunned disbelief through a collection of some twenty thousand stakes, each decorated with the remains of a Turkish prisoner, European renegade, or Christian criminal. For once, silent in the face of a capacity for terror that nearly matched their own, the invaders were badly shaken as they entered this "forest of the impaled."

Mehmet the Conqueror, destroyer of Constantinople and sultan of the mighty Ottoman Empire, had met his match. He had come face to face with Vlad III of Wallachia, more popularly known by the title he inherited from his father, a member of the Dragon Order of Chivalry, Dracula.

After more than five hundred years and diluted by vapid and often puerile novels, films, and other fantasies, the word still inspires dread. Depending on your point of view, however, Vlad III Tepes ("the Impaler") was either not as black as he is painted or much worse. To the surprise of Americans and western Europeans, he is regarded as a national hero in Romania.

This is not to say that Vlad was not a cruel and heartless foe. In justification, he saw himself as a new champion of Christendom against the Ottoman threat.

Having been a hostage of the Turk and having seen what they did to prisoners, Vlad knew what they feared most. He used this knowledge to good effect. He remains the only opponent the Turks ever faced who inspired them with the terror they consistently sought to instill in others.

The Ottomans had been trying to seize control of Wallachia, key to the control of the Balkans, since the early 1400s. A number of attempts to put a Turkish puppet on the throne of the principality had met with failure.

As a buffer zone between the Kingdom of Hungary and the Ottomans, Wallachia had long been the object of a struggle between those two major powers in the Balkans. Not being able to make any headway, the Turks satisfied themselves with levying tribute and otherwise left the country alone.

When it became evident that János Hunyadi, regent ("governor") of Hungary, was growing too powerful for their comfort, however, Sultan Murad released his hostage, Vlad III, and put him on the throne. In response, Hunyadi invaded Wallachia in December 1447, deposed Vlad, and put Vladislav II, possibly his own relative, in Vlad's place.

Some scholars now dispute this, claiming that Hunyadi installed Dan, possibly a son of Basarab II. It is not clear, as records were not well kept at this time and were often based more on rumor than verified facts.

For example, the contemporary Polish chronicler Jan Długosz claimed that Hunyadi had Vlad blinded and planned to take over Wallachia himself. Hunyadi may very well have been planning a coup, but he did not have Vlad blinded.

Far from blind, but definitely out of power, Vlad sought refuge in Moldavia, ruled by his uncle, Bogdan II. Bogdan was assassinated in 1451, however. Preferring to risk trusting a Christian foe rather than a Turkish friend, Vlad went to Hungary to seek sanctuary with Hunyadi.

Realizing the value of Vlad's great knowledge of Ottoman psychology and politics, Hunyadi reconciled his differences with the Wallachian refugee. The fact that Vlad had a virulent hatred of everything Turkish, especially of the new sultan, Mehmet II, only made him more valuable.

Hunyadi offered Vlad a post as advisor, but Vlad refused. This was probably because Vlad planned on eventually retaking Wallachia from one whom he regarded as Hunyadi's creature, and he would not take an oath of fealty to Hunyadi. Vlad's hatred of anything that smacked of disloyalty or treason was at least as great as his loathing of the Turks.

Vlad's chance soon came. In 1456, three years after taking Constantinople, Mehmet II besieged the city of Nándorfehérvár (present day Belgrade) in his campaign to conquer Serbia.

Declaring a Crusade on his own authority, Hunyadi, ably supported on the spiritual side by a Franciscan friar named Giovanni Capistrano (later canonized), launched a counterattack. He lifted the siege but died of the plague soon after, as did Capistrano. With Hunyadi out of the way as protector of Vladislav II, Vlad quickly moved into Wallachia with his own army, killed the man he regarded as a usurper, and reassumed the throne.

Vlad's most famous battle began with the declaration of a Crusade against the Turk by Pope Pius II in 1458.

For years, Hunyadi had urged first Pope Eugene IV, then Pope Nicholas V, and finally Pope Callixtus III to preach a new Crusade. This was on the grounds that it was better to attack than defend, as he had stated in a letter to Nicholas V in 1448.

Callixtus was enthusiastic about the idea, but Emperor Frederick III resisted. At the Imperial Diet (legislature) he convoked to discuss the proposal, Frederick, probably fearful of Hunyadi's wealth, power, and ability, had prevented him from attending.

Despite the usual fervent promises of help from others, nothing was forthcoming, especially from Germany, where generous promises had been made and almost immediately forgotten. While the European powers preferred to struggle amongst themselves, the pope continued to urge men everywhere to unite in the face of a common foe and take the cross.

Pope Pius II succeeded Callixtus in 1458, inheriting not only the See of Saint Peter but also his predecessor's crusading fervor. Still, while the Crusade was never far from Pius's thoughts, it excited very little interest from the rest of Europe. At one point, from 1460 to 1461, the pope was completely abandoned by virtually every Christian power.

Pius II was almost alone in seeing the dangers represented by the Turks. All alone, that is, except for one unimportant prince of an obscure territory near Transylvania, Vlad III of Wallachia. In the winter of 1461–62, Vlad was the only Christian ruler to respond to the pope's declaration of a new Crusade.

Probably because he had regained his throne by his own efforts and felt he owed nothing to the Turks, Vlad had refused to pay tribute for three years. An arrears of thirty thousand ducats (nearly three hundred pounds of gold) had accumulated. Vlad used the money to build up his army and defenses. His intent seems to have been to force Mehmet II either to surrender all claims to Wallachia or undertake an expensive invasion.

From Wallachia, Vlad made lightning strikes all along the Danube, frozen solid in a winter that seemed to break records for subzero temperatures. He attacked towns on the Bulgarian side of the Danube, Bulgaria having recently been added to the Ottoman Empire.

Refused help by the king of Hungary, Mátyás I, son of Hunyadi, Vlad was unable to complete a program of liberation. Instead, large numbers of Bulgarian peasants who wished to remain Christian followed his army back to Wallachia and settled there.

Other Bulgarians, usually of the middle and upper classes, had uttered the "Inshallah" and converted to Islam. Bowing to the conqueror gave them their best, if not only, chance to preserve their wealth and social position. They resisted Vlad's incursions. Vlad captured a number of these apostate Christians and put them to death in the "forest of the impaled" near his capital.

Sickening as this act was, however, the Turks did the same to apostate Muslims. Vlad had an additional incentive in that such individuals could reasonably be construed as traitors politically as well as religiously. They would have constituted a deadly fifth column had he managed to retake Bulgaria as planned.

In another attempt to gain Hungarian support, Vlad sent a letter to Mátyás I demonstrating that he was the equal of the Turks and was openly at war with them. Much of the letter consisted of a list of damages he had inflicted and the number of people he had killed. Vlad destroyed virtually every military or port facility the Turks could have used to launch an offensive up the Danube.

Other reports chronicled numbers killed in battle or executed in various ways. These included a few thousand Turks marched off to Vlad's capital, Tirgoviste, and impaled alongside their recently converted Bulgarian brethren and the odd thief and murderer.

Vlad had thrown down the gauntlet to Mehmet II in the most insulting manner possible. The sultan sent a punitive expedition that captured Braila, the most important Wallachian port on the Danube. The Turkish commander, Mahmud (a Greek/Serbian renegade) then became overconfident and went after Vlad himself with his full force of eighteen thousand troops.

Barely eight thousand survived. The rest, dead or alive, seem to have ended up as ornaments decorating Vlad's "forest of the impaled" along with some Turkish emissaries.

Mehmet had sent the emissaries ostensibly as ambassadors, but in reality, to deliver threats and insults. Vlad used the emissaries' failure to remove their turbans in his presence as a pretext to justify nailing the headgear in place and impaling them—a violation of the sanctity of diplomats that had been observed in various Muslim/Christian encounters in the past. Such niceties were not to be observed in Wallachia.

The conqueror had had enough. The Danube route, firmly under the control of Vlad, was obviously not the optimal way to proceed. The sultan ordered an invasion of Wallachia via the land route through Bulgaria as soon as he was free of his current commitments—extending the Turkish conquest into Asia against both Islamic and the few remaining Christian powers.

Meanwhile, Vlad's praises were being sung throughout Europe. Offers of help again flooded in, especially from Hungary. Ultimately these were to prove as ephemeral as the pledges made to the pope, but they seemed at the time hard evidence that Vlad was succeeding in his goal of kick-starting the new Crusade.

Counting on these promises and knowing all the while that he could not stand alone against the Ottoman Empire, Vlad continued to make preparations to resist. He sent messages to the various European powers, urging them to join him and support Pius's cause.

In order to secure Hungarian help, Vlad agreed to a marriage with a Hungarian princess and the necessary conversion to Latin Christianity. This was not as problematical as it might have been at other times. The Council of Florence in 1439 had arranged another of the transitory unions between the Latin and Greek churches, and it was still in effect. Vlad's conversion was a formality, not the criminal act that Russian sources would later make it out to be.

Vlad insisted that help must be forthcoming by April 23, 1462, the Feast of Saint George. He also sent envoys to Armenia, Georgia, the Khan of Crim Tartary (Crimea), and the Genoese colony of Caffa, all of which were threatened by Mehmet.

None of this desperately needed aid materialized. Nevertheless, Vlad continued his preparations to resist the Turkish onslaught that he knew had to come the moment that the sultan finished his campaign in Anatolia. The only assistance Vlad received was in the form of some instructions by Mátyás I to the Hungarian garrison at Chilia to assist Vlad should the fortress be attacked. This rather watery response by Mátyás I is explained by the fact that he obviously expected Vlad to secure his border against the Turks for him.

In any event, Mátyás I was preparing to face off against the Emperor Frederick III in case that ruler should fail to turn the crown of Saint Stephen over to him. Lukewarm as was Mátyás's response to Vlad, it justified the king's acceptance of a papal subsidy and crusading funds and their use in strengthening defenses . . . on the western side of the country against fellow Christians instead of the Turk.

In the meantime, Mehmet II finished a campaign in Asia. He was now free to devote his full attention to other matters. He set out from Istanbul on May 17, 1462, with virtually the whole of his army. The importance he put on crushing the upstart prince of Wallachia is demonstrated by the fact that the sultan took personal command of the expedition.

Mehmet did not seek merely to punish Vlad, however. His goal was to take over Wallachia as a Turkish province and provide a steppingstone to the conquest of Europe. Vlad, unlike other contemporary rulers, seems to have realized the seriousness of the Ottoman threat and was prepared to take any and all measures to resist it.

The number of men the sultan mustered varies according to who did the counting. The Greek historian Chalcondyles claimed that the expedition was at least as large as that which had taken Constantinople less than a decade earlier. He estimated its size at 250,000.

Turun Bey, the Turkish historian, put the number at three hundred thousand. Tommasi, the Venetian envoy at Buda, the Hungarian capital, stated that Mehmet had assembled a force of regulars of sixty thousand, plus irregular levies of twenty to thirty thousand.

Who is right? Probably all three. Turkish expeditionary forces consisted of a core of regulars, possibly the finest soldiers and the best equipped of any in the world at the time. These janissaries (infantry) and *sipahis* (feudal levies of cavalry) were summoned at the sultan's command for the annual campaigning season by the raising of the *Tug*, the horsetail standard.

A janissary was a member of the elite military units of the Turkish army, organized by Sultan Murad I around 1375. Today connoting any member of a group of loyal guards, soldiers, or supporters, the corps was originally composed of kidnapped Christian boys forced to convert to Islam.

Janissaries were slaves, but paid a salary and given frequent gifts as well as sharing in the loot from military campaigns. In order to ensure their complete loyalty to the sultan, they were forbidden to marry or engage in trade.

Over time, the corps lost its military character as civilians purchased memberships in order to obtain the benefits of being an official slave of the state. When Sultan Murad II modernized the military in 1826, the janissaries revolted in "the Auspicious (or Unfortunate) Event." More than six thousand janissaries were executed, and the corps disbanded. At this time, however, the janissaries were a force to be reckoned with and considered some of the finest soldiers in the world, albeit often poorly led. To the janissaries and *sipahis* were added irregular volunteers willing to fight for loot and slaves and a huge contingent of conscripts and slaves to carry out siege operations. Such cannon fodder usually outnumbered actual fighters by a factor of about 1½. A force with about 100,000 combatants would, therefore, contain about 150,000 of these "engineers," who typically died by the tens of thousands in a siege.

Artillery was the most fearsome part of the Ottoman force. Mehmet brought what must have amounted to his entire arsenal on the expedition, at least 120 heavy guns. These, designed and manufactured by a Hungarian renegade, had turned the tide at the final siege of Constantinople. They were to form the core of Turkish strength for the next century or so until Western technology caught up with and ultimately surpassed that of the East.

Valuable as such ordnance was in an assault on fixed fortifications, however, it was to prove a handicap against a Wallachian prince fighting what amounted to a guerrilla war. Effective mobile field artillery was still centuries in the future.

The enormous siege pieces tended to bog down rapidly in the sticky soil, dark forests, and swampy ground of eastern Europe. They were almost completely useless on the campaign and acted as a brake on the speed of the columns. The *ceausi,* or "ushers," attempted to keep things moving by plying their whips on the troops and ordering the occasional judicious beheading, but progress remained slow.

Mehmet's force was supported by a fleet of approximately 150 ships, which, had things gone according to plan, were to range up and down the Danube attacking various concentrations of power. Due to Vlad's earlier destruction of virtually everything along the river, however, these proved to be singularly ineffective. They confined themselves to attacks on Braila and Chilia. They were most useful afterwards in facilitating the withdrawal of the sultan's troops.

Against this fighting machine, Vlad was able to field an estimated thirty thousand, of which twenty-two thousand were poorly equipped infantry, mostly peasant levies and volunteers, and eight thousand cavalry of the boyar (land-owning) class, armed in the traditional medieval fashion with sword and lance. Vlad also had an efficient spy organization composed primarily of Gypsies, who gained pardon for crimes so long as they remained in his service.

With the help of this secret service, Vlad was able to plan a series of meticulously detailed raids. Unlike some such efforts, these hit-and-run attacks against Turkish camps or stragglers were extremely effective. They gained their immediate goal of killing as many Turks as possible and slowed the advance of the Ottoman army.

Contrary to the Dracula of legend, Vlad seemed to have an innate ability to inspire extraordinary loyalty in his followers. Morale was very high, and Vlad constantly exhorted his troops to the heights of bravery, some might say to the point of foolhardiness. In sharp contrast to the Turkish soldiers, who sometimes had to be driven to battle with whips, Vlad informed his men that those who were afraid of death should not follow him.

Clearly Vlad wanted no unwilling men filling his ranks. Once there, however, the men were expected to fight. He would examine the wounds of his men after an engagement. Those with wounds in front were rewarded. Those with wounds in back were impaled for their presumed cowardice. Apparently the number of such executions was not high.

Vlad's effectiveness and popularity as a leader is demonstrated by the fact that he managed to raise what amounted to a mass levy of the male population of fighting age in his Crusade against the invader, possibly close to 20 percent of the entire population. Other countries—usually to their later sorrow—were to experience mass desertions to the enemy when the Ottomans invaded.

During the advance, the sultan captured one of Vlad's peasant raiders. Unable to break him by either threats or promises of reward, Mehmet finally hinted that the man's end was near via some more than ordinarily horrifying tortures. The peasant is said to have replied that he knew he was completely at the sultan's mercy, but whatever Mehmet did to him, he would never betray Dracula.

The sultan, at first angry, finally admitted that if Vlad had many more soldiers like the peasant, he could conquer the world in a very short time. It is not recorded whether the peasant's life was spared.

Finally Mehmet was able to make Vlad and his army stand and fight. The Turks forced a crossing of the Danube at Turnu, on the Romanian side of the river. Vlad had inflicted heavy damage on this port, but it was still serviceable. By sailing up the Ort River, Mehmet would be within striking distance of Vlad's capital of Tirgoviste.

On the night of Friday, June 4, 1462, the sultan's janissaries crossed the river in seventy barges and, for once, took Vlad by surprise. They had floated down the river to a point several kilometers below where Vlad's army had taken up its position. To guard against an assault by the Wallachian cavalry, which had already put several scares into the Turkish ranks, they dug entrenchments. They then crossed back over the river and brought in more janissaries as well as what artillery they could muster.

The janissaries then advanced on Vlad's camp and began to site the guns. By now, the Wallachian force was alerted and managed to account for an estimated three hundred Turks. Mehmet, watching the fight from the other side of the river, was pushed to the edge of anxiety by this unexpected turn of events. He considered ordering a retreat lest his entire janissary corps be wiped out.

By that time, however, the Turks managed to bring all of their guns into play and were able to stave off Vlad's counterattack. Instantly realizing the futility of storming fixed gun emplacements, the Wallachian prince ordered a withdrawal.

Mehmet then felt it was safe enough to cross the river and join his men. He proclaimed a great victory and distributed largesse to the troops to the tune of thirty thousand ducats—the amount of tribute Vlad was in arrears.

The drawn out battle now entered a second phase. Vlad retreated deeper into his own territory to gain tactical advantage, while Mehmet followed to try and effect his total destruction. Adding to the sultan's superiority was the fact that he had Vlad's brother, Radu, commanding four thousand *sipahis*, ready and willing to take over the principality in exchange for subjugating it completely to the Turks.

Despite the ascendance enjoyed by the sultan, Vlad did not make his advance into Wallachia easy. The terrain itself acted as a powerful defense. The swampy ground, sheer mountains, and the thick forest of Vlasia all combined to make physical movement of an army difficult.

It did not help Mehmet's army any when Vlad had a number of streams and small rivers dammed to create instant marshes in the path of the invaders. The women and children hid out in the middle of these swamps, while the men took up residence in the dark woods from which neighboring Transylvania, "Across the Woods," gets its name. From there, they made guerrilla strikes at the sultan's forces. These were combined with attacks from Vlad's now somewhat depleted main force, one of them led by Vlad himself.

Added to that was Vlad's policy of leaving nothing behind for the invaders, man or beast, to eat or drink. He ordered crops burned, wells poisoned, and any cattle slaughtered that could not keep up with the march.

As Vlad's tiny army withdrew to his capital, towns and villages were depopulated. People fled and hid, or followed their prince in order to avoid the horrors that traditionally accompanied a Turkish invasion.

Vlad even reinvented an old trick from Roman and Greek days, attempting to infect the invading horde with every possible disease. He offered a bounty to anyone with a terminal illness, leprosy, tuberculosis, and, especially, the Black Death to mingle with and, if opportunity permitted, embrace as many Turks as possible. Survivors were richly rewarded. Plague eventually swept through the Turkish ranks. Hardened criminals were also pardoned on condition that they kill as many stragglers as they could find. In view of the lack of forage, the only possible way for Mehmet to advance on Vlad's capital was to make a great detour around the city, coming from the north instead of the south. After all the delays, Vlad finally made a desperate night attack. Had his allies followed through or if the Wallachian prince had just a little more luck, the career of Mehmet II would have ended on June 17, 1462, in a chase after someone he regarded as little better than a bandit.

Vlad and his army, now numbering approximately twenty-four thousand, had been cornered in an almost inaccessible mountain pass. Mehmet besieged him and sat down to wait for Vlad either to starve or surrender.

Vlad did neither. Knowing the deep fears the Turks entertained about spirits (considered by some authorities to be the reason for so few night attacks by Ottoman troops), Vlad planned an after-dark attack to take out the sultan and end the invasion by cutting off the head of the snake.

Carefully dividing his troops and, to his later misfortune, command of the army, Vlad positioned his men around the Turkish camp. He put a boyar by the name of Gales in charge of the other division with instructions to press forward when the Turks were confused and catch them between the upper and nether millstones.

This would, presumably, clear the way to the ultimate goal, the man inhabiting the tent of the sultan. Vlad's men were ordered to kill Mehmet on sight. In keeping with the focused objective, which had the best chance of success, Vlad himself led the charge into the Turkish camp.

At first, things could not have gone better. Chaos seemed to spread rapidly throughout the camp, with milling bands of Turks running headlong into Wallachian attack squads.

Things were not as confused as Vlad could have wished, however. The Turks, especially the janissaries, were superbly trained. Despite the panic and confusion surrounding them, most of them stood their ground and stayed at their posts.

This would have been the right time for Gales to make his sortie, taking the Turks from the rear. For some reason never explained, however, he withdrew without taking any effective action. A Turkish eyewitness to the attack declared that if Gales had been as audacious as Vlad the Devil, the Wallachians would have carried the day.

A second error now occurred. There was still a good chance of assassinating Mehmet, but the Wallachians, misdirected by some Turks they had captured and questioned, zeroed in on the tent of the sultan's two viziers instead of that of the sultan himself. This gave the Turks time to regroup and arrange a cavalry charge as well as position Mehmet's crack division of janissaries around his tent.

Realizing the attack was a failure, Vlad retreated. Mehmet ordered pursuit, but the Turks were by this time so unnerved by Vlad's tactics that it petered out. An estimated two thousand Wallachians were taken prisoner, and Vlad himself may have been wounded. The Wallachian prince may have lost as many as five thousand men, while the Turks lost a possible fifteen thousand in the ill-fated "Night of Attack."

Vlad now barricaded himself and his army in his capital of Tirgoviste, which became Mehmet's target.

Accounts differ at this point. One source asserts that, having fortified his city for a prolonged siege, Vlad suddenly abandoned Tirgoviste and absconded with the entire population, leaving the gates open to the Turks. Mehmet later came across the infamous "forest of the impaled."

Confusing two campaigns, the story is that the sultan was so shocked by such barbarism that he immediately placed Vlad's brother "Radu the Handsome," who had shared the Ottoman ruler's bed on a number of occasions, on the throne. He then hunted Vlad down and killed him.

The most consistent account, however, holds that the advance guard of the Turkish army came upon the execution ground a few days after the Night of Attack but before reaching the capital. This was probably June 19 or 20. The sultan was sent for, and, far from reacting in revulsion (one account has the Turks rolling on the ground and vomiting in fear and horror), he seems to have expressed admiration for a foe who, while a hostage, had obviously learned Ottoman terror tactics all too well.

Admiration, but also apprehension. Vlad was a master of psychological warfare. He knew that the tactics used by the Turks were those they themselves feared. Modern accounts gloss over the fact that the Turks had already developed and perfected every act Vlad carried out.

That night, Mehmet gave orders for an especially deep trench to be dug around the Turkish camp. The next day he ordered a retreat. Vlad had won—for the time being.

Later, after the immediate threat of Turkish invasion was gone, Vlad was deposed after some convoluted power politics. Tired of his policies, which seemed to bring them nothing but war and hardship, and now safe from the immediate threat, the common people failed to rise up and support him.

Nevertheless, Vlad III succeeded in one of his goals. Wallachia was autonomous and would remain so, although still tributary to the Ottoman Empire. Had he not carried out what amounted to a one-man Crusade, Wallachia would have been integrated into the empire and provided a steppingstone to the goal that was to elude every Ottoman sultan: Vienna, the heart of Europe.

Had Vlad succeeded in his attempt to kill Mehmet on the Night of Attack, it is probable that Pius's Crusade would have received an enormous impetus. Constantinople, held by then for less than a decade, could have been retaken and, from there, the rest of Asia Minor. The "Terrible Turk" would have become a distant memory.

It was not until a year after the momentum of Vlad's campaign had petered out that anyone else responded to Pius's call. The pope invited all the Christian nobility to join, and the Venetians responded, as did George Kastriot Skanderbeg, the leader of Albanian resistance.

On November 27, 1463, Skanderbeg declared war on the Ottomans and attacked their forces near Ohrid. Pius II envisioned assembling twenty thousand soldiers in Taranto, while Skanderbeg would gather an equal number. The plan was to rendezvous in Durazzo under Skanderbeg's leadership and present a solid, united front against the Ottomans.

Pius II even prepared a letter to Mehmet II. It contained a detailed refutation of the Quran, an exposition of the Christian faith, and an appeal to the sultan to forsake

Islam, accept baptism, and take up the crown of the Eastern Empire. The letter was probably never sent, although some historians believe it might have been . . . to no effect. The pope succeeded in bringing together Holy Roman Emperor Frederick III and King Mátyás I "the Just" of Hungary, the son of János Hunyadi and Elisabeth Szilágyi. The discovery of alum deposits in Tolfa in the Papal States provided the necessary financing.

Unfortunately, King Louis XI of France, "the Universal Spider," was unwilling to undertake any project not to his advantage or that of the realm. Louis did, however, give Philip III, Duke of Burgundy, four hundred thousand gold crowns to carry out a Crusade in exchange for a number of Burgundian territories.

This outraged Philip's son Charles, the future Charles the Bold, who felt he was being robbed of his inheritance. Charles joined a rebellion against Louis led by the king's brother, Charles, Duke of Berry, which put an end to the possibility of any help from Burgundy. Milan and Genoa were at war with one another, while the Florentines advised the pope to let their rivals the Venetians and the Turks destroy each other.

Pius II, debilitated by illness and with his judgment probably impaired as a result, waited until June 1464. He then decided to assume personal command, took the cross, and traveled to Ancona.

The Venetian fleet was delayed, and most of the army melted away. When the Venetian ships finally arrived, the pope was too ill to do anything other than view them from the window of his sick room. He died two days later, August 14, 1464.

HISTORICAL NOTE: REALITY TO MYTH

How did a national hero ever become branded one of the greatest monsters in human history, not to mention achieve immortality as a blood-sucking undead creature of the night? We can probably blame it on early mass media. Most of what is popularly known about Vlad III Tepes, "the Impaler," appears to have its roots in a very effective propaganda campaign.

By modern standards, Vlad was a cruel and inhumanly harsh ruler. He was not, however, seen as tyrannical by most of his subjects. They had the undeniable oppression carried out by the Turks too close at hand for them to have any illusions as to what constituted real horror.

This was not true of the German Saxons who inhabited the northern part of Vlad's domain, protected to a certain extent from Turkish depredations. The battle of Tannenberg (1410), in which the Slavs and Balts defeated the Teutonic Knights, was within living memory. Vlad's Saxon subjects carried on the by-then traditional animosity of Teuton against Slav. They considered themselves oppressed by the mere fact that Vlad was not German.

Saxon hatred of their suzerain was expressed in what was to become classic Germanic fashion. Pamphlets containing various anecdotes and woodcuts, the equivalent of today's editorial cartoons, purporting to show (among other revolting acts) Vlad feasting among or even on the bodies of his impaled victims, circulated widely.

Almost as much as now, people put more credence in the written word than the spoken word. The Bible, after all, was the most widespread writing available in the late

Middle Ages, particularly in Germany, with more than seventy full translations of the Bible in prior to 1500, and countless selections from the Gospels and Psalms. All writing prior to the modern denigration of the Bible and the antics of yellow journalists tended to acquire a little of the distinction of Holy Writ by the mere fact of being writing. Anti-Vlad propaganda had enormous authority simply by appearing in written form.

Unfortunately for historical accuracy, these pamphlets tend to be a little surreal and do not match well (or at all) with known facts. Anecdotes are related in a way that calls to mind the folk tales gathered by the Brothers Grimm. They usually open with some phrase that can be translated into English as, "Once upon a time . . ."; and this when Vlad was still among the living.

One villainy, at least, that cannot be laid at the feet of Vlad III, according to Elizabeth Miller, professor of English at Memorial University, Newfoundland, is inspiring Anglo-Irish author Bram Stoker's (in)famous hero. According to Dr. Miller, Stoker took nothing more than the name "Dracula" from Romania's national hero.

As with most folk tales, however, there generally is some grain of truth in the stories. Vlad was unbelievably harsh to malefactors, although had he killed as many of his own subjects as legend or pamphlet relate, he would not have had any subjects left.

The total population of Wallachia in the mid-fifteenth century was anywhere from 100,000 to 250,000, less than some of the numbers that Vlad is supposed to have had killed. One presumably moderate source reports that he

slaughtered "between 40 and 100 thousand." This is a substantial differential even for an estimate.

Many, but not all, criminals were impaled, this being a
punishment Vlad had learned from the Turks. The fact that
Vlad was able to empty his prisons to gain recruits for his
Crusade argues against the draconian law enforcement with
which even serious histories credit him. If anyone guilty
of any crime, no matter how minor, was impaled, where
did the "hardened criminals" come from to gain pardon
by attacking Mehmet? Other anecdotes have even bigger
holes in them.

Except for what he inflicted on Turks and criminals, very
little credence can therefore be placed in the numerous stories of tortures Vlad presumably meted out. For Turks and
criminals there are usually names, dates, and places, a more
reliable reporting format than a folk tale or propaganda
pamphlet.

On the other hand, there is well-corroborated evidence of
atrocities that appear to have been inspired by the fictional
Vlad whose story was spread through early mass media. At
about the same time that "Dracula" was crusading against
the Turk, England was in the throes of the dynastic conflict
later known as the Wars of the Roses.

Just as Vlad was faced by treachery from within and
without, Edward IV of the House of York had to deal with
a great many Lancastrian plots against his throne. The man
he chose to search out and destroy conspirators was one
John Tiptoft, Earl of Worcester. Tiptoft is one of the most
repulsive figures in English history and considered by some
to be the model, with Henry VII, for the title character in
Shakespeare's *Richard III*.

Sometime around 1465, Tiptoft began a reign of terror in England, executing conspirators and alleged conspirators in various creative ways, often without the formality of a trial. A favorite form of execution used by Tiptoft was the previously unheard-of method of impalement. While on a level with the traditional English punishment of hanging, drawing, and quartering, its very novelty ensured a greater air of horror, which Tiptoft apparently considered necessary to maintain his power base.

Tiptoft was—perhaps paradoxically, perhaps not, given what we have seen done by many well-educated men in recent centuries—one of the most learned men in England. His translations of various classics from the Latin were among the first works printed in England. He was aware of the intellectual and technical innovations taking place in Europe. He could not have failed to come across samples of the new printing process in the form of the German pamphlets published against Vlad III.

These described in graphic detail the tortures the Wallachian prince allegedly inflicted on his own people. The myth built up around Vlad touched a chord in Tiptoft's sadistic soul, and he adopted parts of the program.

Later, when Henry VII usurped the throne from Richard III, the Tudor was faced with the problem of blackening the name of the last Plantagenet. Like Vlad, Richard was extremely popular with the common people. He had been perceived as their champion against the greed of the various factions surrounding his brother, Edward IV, and that of foreign adventurers such as the "Welsh milksop," Henry Tudor.

Henry, although a hanger-on at the court of Brittany, had been at the center of European intrigue almost from his birth. He could not help but be aware of Vlad's career—and how his reputation had been ruined by the German propaganda campaign. Cannier than most, Henry did not make the mistake of committing his accusations against Richard to print in anything other than vague form. There were too many people who knew the truth, and they all could not be silenced. Alleged facts would have been checked and publicized. Rumor was far more effective than the written word.

It was not until the reign of Henry VIII that memories began fading and "facts" about Richard could be asserted without too much fear of contradiction that the Black Legend of Richard really took off. This was sufficiently egregious that Thomas More began a satire on Henry VII, assigning acts of the first Tudor to the last Plantagenet and adding ridiculous details to make certain that no one took the characterization seriously.

Even so, the picture was obviously that of Henry VII rather than Richard III, and More abandoned the project. The Tudor police state was no place to mock a ruler, at least in any recognizable form.

More took up the task later and lampooned the Tudors and their new style of government in *Utopia*, one of the great seminal works of satire on the totalitarian state. Ironically, many people today take the unfinished "history" of Richard III and *Utopia* as historical fact and a blueprint for an ideal society, respectively! It is as if future generations will view *Mad* magazine and George Orwell's *1984* as serious journalism and a recommendation for social restructuring.

Similarly, when living memory of Vlad III faded, "authoritative sources" in the form of the German propaganda pamphlets and folk tales formed opinion in the West. Since western European historians generally have not gone to eastern European sources—which usually depict Vlad as a hero rather than a monster—the picture that comes down to us is based on flawed assumptions.

Add to that the typical Western academic's distaste for European culture and civilization and the consequent promotion of the Islamic side of the issue. (When, after all, was the last time you read anything good about the Crusades?) Given that disreputable mix, you have the perfect recipe for creating an inhuman fiend almost out of whole cloth.

3

MOHÁCS

1526

THE failure of the West to follow up on the momentum of Vlad III's Crusade and Pius II's call for another was to have tragic consequences. In partial extenuation of this setback, the death of both János Hunyadi and Saint Giovanni Capistrano within a few months of one another after relieving the siege of Nándorfehérvár, which many believe to have been Hunyadi's greatest victory, had thrown the entire region into chaos.

Ladislas V of Hungary, an extraordinarily weak and inexperienced king, added serious moral failings to the disadvantage of youth. One historian described him as being at the age of seventeen "a debauched, neurotic lout."

During the struggle between the rival Cillei and Hunyadi factions for power, supporters of Hunyadi murdered Ulric Cillei. The king arrested both of Hunyadi's sons and beheaded the elder, Lázló, in 1457.

Ladislas then fled in panic to Vienna, taking with him Lázló's younger brother, Mátyás, as hostage. There he died of the plague a short time later, and the nobility elected Mátyás king in his place.

Mátyás ruled reasonably well, if somewhat autocratically, until his death in 1490. Pulled in different directions

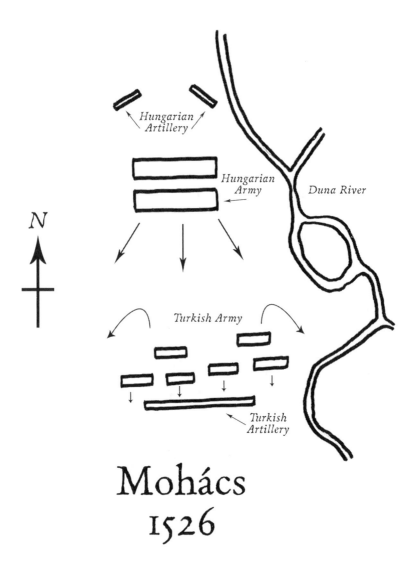

N

Hungarian
Artillery

Hungarian
Army

Duna River

Turkish Army

*Turkish
Artillery*

Mohács
1526

by the complex imperial politics of the time and unable to secure his base, however, he neither assisted Vlad III nor fulfilled his dream of completing his father's campaign against the Turk.

Many historians believe that if Mátyás had not had designs on the throne of Bohemia and even that of the Holy Roman Empire, he would have been successful in uniting the European powers against the Turk and in retaking Constantinople. As it was, his ambitions made potential allies suspicious. With some justification, they assumed that a successful Crusade against the common enemy would put Mátyás in a position of being able to impose his will on them.

When Mátyás died without legitimate issue, the country again fell into chaos. Mátyás had made an effort to legitimize his natural son, János, but failed. An understanding with Emperor Maximilian to assume the throne also fell through.

Finally, the nobility chose Wladislas II Jagiello, king of Bohemia, correctly assuming they could easily control him. Maximilian agreed with the choice of the nobles, on condition that the Austrian provinces formerly held by Mátyás were restored to imperial control.

With the country dissolving in internecine strife, the Turks began making probing raids into the border territories. Clearly something had to be done to resist them.

To gain his support against the nobility, Wladislas made Archbishop Tamás Bakócz his chancellor. With a ruthlessness that matched his intelligence, however, Bakócz used his position to increase his own wealth and power, alienating both the nobility and the common people. Without the support of the nobility against the commons, or that of the commons against the nobility, Wladislas became completely ineffectual.

Making the situation worse, in the conclave that followed the death of Pope Julius II in 1513, Bakócz had arrived with "wagons fully loaded with gold" to ensure his election to the See of Peter. The cardinals, however, honoring Julius's strict ban on simony, elected Giovanni de' Medici, second son of Lorenzo the Magnificent, who took the name Leo X. The new pope proclaimed a Crusade against the Turk. As a sop to the Hungarians and to get rid of Bakócz, Leo commissioned Bakócz to lead the effort.

As with so many of the Medici pope's acts, the choice proved to be extraordinarily unfortunate. The Franciscans charged with recruiting turned out to be an offshoot of the *Fraticelli*, a renegade sect of the Order of the Friars Minor that rejected religious and civil authority and demanded the abolition of private property.

Tens of thousands of disaffected peasants and middle class artisans and merchants, nearly one hundred thousand in all, took the cross. A member of the minor nobility, György Székely (Dózsa), became commander-in-chief, and the first contingent set out in the spring of 1514 across the Great Plain of Hungary.

Given the rhetoric used by the Franciscans in recruiting, the nobility were uncertain whether they or the Turks were the real targets of the Crusade. They forced the king and Bakócz to order the peasant army to disperse by May 15 . . . after it was already on the march.

Blocked in their advance by the rich and powerful John Zápolya, voivode[5] of Transylvania, the army turned back. Due to lack of supplies, a desire for revenge against the nobility, or both, the peasants soon became a disorganized mob, looting and plundering their way across the country. By July 1514, what had turned from a Crusade against the Turk into a peasant revolt against the nobility had been quelled. The legislature enacted harsh laws effectively revoking the peasants' free status and reinstituting serfdom, laws in force until the Revolutions of 1848 brought even more drastic changes to the face of Europe. The peasants became outcasts in their own country, a development for which they were themselves largely responsible.

The defeat of the peasant army did not bring a halt to the conflict between the nobility, headed by John Zápolya, and King Wladislas and Archbishop Bákocz. To counter the growing power of the nobility, Wladislas and Bákocz concluded a succession agreement with the Austrian Hapsburgs.

On the king's death in 1516, his son Louis II became king and married Maria of Habsburg, sister of Emperor Charles V, whose other brother, Archduke Ferdinand, then married Louis's relative Anna Jagiello. This gave Ferdinand a claim to the Hungarian throne by marriage should Louis die without issue.

Ferdinand and Anna's marriage violated the 1505 law restricting the succession to a native Hungarian. The animosity between the "Court faction" (the party of nobles

---

5   An eastern European title for a local ruler or governor, especially in Wallachia, Transylvania, and Moldova, meaning "war leader." Cf. "Duke," from *ducis bellorum*, Latin for "war leader."

around the king) and the "National faction" (the nobility supporting the Zápolya family) became more pronounced than ever. Nor could the international situation be ignored. By 1520, the Turks had begun raids in force, capturing a number of fortresses in Bosnia and Dalmatia in what is now the southernmost portion of Croatia. The new sultan, Süleymân II, to be known in the West as Süleymân the Magnificent, demanded tribute from Louis, but was refused.

On Archbishop Bákocz's death in 1521, István Báthori, the wealthiest man in Hungary after the Zápolya family, became head of the Court faction and chancellor. Soon, however, the minor nobility headed by the jurist István Werböczy of the National faction ousted Báthori.

Werböczy's first act as chancellor was to deprive the powerful Fugger bankers of their Hungarian mining leases. An attempt to remove foreign influences and secure the power of the National faction, the effort backfired.

The Fuggers had paid the miners well, while the government did not pay them at all, evidently considering their labor as feudal dues. The miners rebelled, but were crushed by Werböczy.

In retaliation, the Fuggers cut off credit. Added to the virtual anarchy that ruled the country, this made it impossible for the country to prepare to face the growing Turkish threat. . . .

THE TOMB OF HUNGARY

One of the most serious problems facing any dictatorship is placating the military *élite* so essential to retaining power.

The caesars had their Praetorian guard, the shah of Persia had his Ten Thousand Immortals, while the Ottoman sultans had their janissaries.

When the ruler's *élite* force depends directly on the ruler for its compensation, it is usually good for the ruler and bad for the state and the people—witness the tribulations suffered by the Roman *res publica* as contending *imperatori* who paid their own troops fought for the purple. When the army depends on loot for its pay, however, it can ultimately be bad for everyone.

In early spring of 1525, the Ottoman sultan Süleymân the Magnificent was faced with a mutiny of his janissaries. These belligerent, privileged infantrymen counted on annual campaigns to satisfy their lust not only for battle but for the traditional perquisite of loot.

There had not been a campaign since the 1522 conquest of the island of Rhodes, held by the Knights of Saint John, today known as the Knights of Malta. The Knights, however, had negotiated terms, and there had been virtually no pillaging.

Süleymân's Rhodian campaign had vindicated Mehmet II's failed siege of the island in 1480, nothing more. The sultan needed a new campaign to carry out the Ottoman version of jihad, add new territory to the empire, and replenish his own coffers.

And he had to satisfy his janissaries, who resented the sultan's prolonged inaction.

This was a perennial problem for every Ottoman sultan. The janissaries were growing more powerful every year. They were also growing more aware of their own power, especially since they now formed as much as a quarter of the sultan's standing army. In wartime, these slave soldiers were generally devoted and loyal servants of their master. True, they might disobey the sultan's orders against plundering captured cities, and on occasion limit his conquests by protesting against the continuation of unduly arduous campaigns. In peacetime, however, they tended to grow restless from inaction. When not subject to strict field discipline, they had a habit of turning from the sultan's greatest asset to his greatest liability.

This was especially the case during the interregnum between the death of one sultan and the accession of another. The janissaries had come to regard this as a period of license until their new master took over the reins of government and put them in the way of gaining loot.

In the spring of 1525, the janissaries rioted. They targeted the Jewish quarter and the homes of senior government officials and wealthy merchants.

A group of mutineers even forced their way into the presence of Süleymân himself. Legend has it he himself killed three of them until he was obliged to withdraw when the others threatened his life.

Only the execution of the janissaries' Agha (the official directly in charge) and that of a number of officers suspected of aiding and abetting the rioters restored order. Many others were relieved of command. The janissaries themselves were placated with gifts of money and the promise of a new campaign the following spring.

Süleymân decided on a Hungarian campaign probably because he wanted to follow up on the capture of

Nándorfehérvár (Belgrade) in 1521, interrupted by the siege of Rhodes, which had opened up the Danube as a route of conquest into the heart of Europe. Plus, the situation in Hungary, where virtual anarchy ruled, was custom made for his program of conquest. The country was ripe for the plucking.

The janissary revolt probably hastened Süleymân's decision to march into Hungary, but it was clear that he had marked the country down for conquest some time before. A further incentive was provided by the fact that Emperor Charles V had captured King Francis I of France at the battle of Pavia in 1525.

Imprisoned in Madrid, Francis opened up secret communication with Süleymân. The French king pleaded with the sultan to attack Charles, who might otherwise become ruler of the entire world.

Süleymân, however, could not attack Vienna without first securing Hungary . . . which fitted nicely into his plans. He recalled Ibrahim Pasha from Egypt and made him military commander of the Ottoman imperial forces, effectively second-in-command after Süleymân.

Rather than simply invade Hungary, however, Süleymân set to work legitimizing the campaign. This was essential, for even had the Turkish forces conquered the entire country or even occupied it without fighting, they could not have held it.

Hungary was a salient deep into what for the Ottomans was enemy territory and at the extreme end of the line of communication from Istanbul. The ideal outcome for Süleymân was not direct rule but submission and the erection of a puppet government under Ottoman control.

With a weak king and the nobility of the Court faction at odds with the National faction under the leadership of John Zápolya, the situation could not have been better for the sultan. Louis II and the Court faction supported Charles V, but received nothing in return, particularly in the form of help against the machinations of the National faction.

Süleymân could present himself as supporting John Zápolya, the presumably legitimate (albeit unelected) king under the succession law of 1505. At the same time, he could pose as the deliverer of the peasants whose liberties had been revoked following the Crusade-turned-rebellion of 1514.

Finally, on April 23, 1526, Süleymân the Magnificent, sultan of the Ottoman Empire, set out for Hungary. Accompanying him was an army of approximately one hundred thousand men, half of whom were battle-hardened professionals, and a siege train of three hundred pieces of heavy artillery, with additional ordnance picked up from depots along the way.

Despite the intensive preparation, progress was slow after leaving the neighborhood of Nándorfehérvár, where the local rulers were also obligated to keep the roads in good shape. This was despite the fact that Süleymân had sent Ibrahim, in whom he had complete confidence, ahead to smooth the way whenever the invaders anticipated difficulties.

There had been some benefits too, however. When the army arrived at Nándorfehérvár, Ibrahim had already constructed a bridge across the Suva, a tributary of the Danube.

The Serbians had retreated to the north bank of the Danube but left a garrison at the citadel of the city of

Peterwarden on the south bank. The sultan commanded Ibrahim to take the town, declaring that it would only whet his appetite until he could have his breakfast in Vienna. Ibrahim took the town quickly, putting most of the garrison to the sword after surrender and enslaving the rest.

Anticipating that the Hungarians' first line of defense would be at the River Drava, another tributary of the Danube, the Ottoman army marched west along the river. Much to Süleymân's and Ibrahim's surprise, however, the north bank of the Drava had been left undefended. Even in the face of the enemy, the Hungarians had not been able to resolve their differences and organize an effective defense—or any defense at all.

The town of Essek on the south bank of the Drava, left without recourse, submitted to Süleymân without a fight. He then ordered a pontoon bridge be thrown across the river, completing a job that his engineers had estimated would take three months in just three days. After getting his army across the river, he then ordered the bridge destroyed to ensure that the soldiers of his army knew their choice was victory or death.

Despite such engineering miracles, progress was slow, and some equipment had to be left behind. Once past Nándorfehérvár, there were no bridges, and roads were virtually non-existent. In addition, the spring of 1526 had seen exceptionally heavy rainfall. The Danube and its tributaries were in high flood, and what passed for roads were muddy traps for the Turkish cannon and other equipment.

The large fleet of vessels the governor of Nándorfehérvár had assembled for Süleymân to transport equipment up the river could make almost no headway, and efforts to construct temporary bridges met with no success in most instances. The army proceeded at a snail's pace.

Nor did the weather improve. Torrential rains and even hailstorms continued into the summer. Streams were virtually impassable. They overflowed their banks, sweeping away bridges and camps and flooding roads.

Nature was putting up a more effective resistance to the invader than the Hungarians. Had they managed to come together and engage the Turks on their march, it is highly probable the Hungarians would have inflicted serious damage, possibly even forcing the enemy to turn back.

Finally, however, the Hungarians under Louis II began assembling on the plain of Mohács, approximately fifty or so kilometers north of the Turkish position. Starting with barely four thousand men, the Hungarian army swelled to an unimpressive twenty-five thousand. Many of these were not even Hungarians, but Poles, Bohemians, and Germans.

Charles V, Holy Roman emperor, was hamstrung in attempting to send reinforcements. The Protestant Diets with which he had to deal were reluctant to vote men, money, and material to fight the Turks when they viewed the pope as a greater threat—and had the opportunity to let the Turks and the Catholics eliminate each other. The Diet of Speyer would finally vote for aid after long negotiations . . . too late to do any good.

With their army (such as it was) outnumbered four to one, fewer than two dozen cannon, and in a bad tactical position, wiser heads among the Hungarians suggested a strategic retreat back to the capital, Buda. Presumably this would recreate the earlier situation that the Hungarians had failed to exploit by lengthening the Turkish lines of communication and making it impossible for the Turks to concentrate their forces to ward off any attack. It would also allow time for additional reinforcements to gather. John Zápolya's army of ten thousand troops was only a few days march away, and there was word that another Bohemian contingent had crossed the western frontier.

For some reason, however, the native Magyar nobility of Hungary held the Turks in contempt and also had visions of the glory that would be theirs for defeating the seemingly unconquerable Ottoman host without help. They also distrusted the king and were suspicious of John Zápolya.

Whether out of inexperience, a similar desire for glory, or fear of appearing to be a coward, Louis decided to stand and fight. In order to maximize the advantage of the heavily armored Hungarian cavalry, the swampy plain of Mohács in front of the town of the same name, west of the Danube, was chosen.

That Mohács gave even greater advantage to the far more numerous and lightly armored *sipahis*, less likely to get bogged down in the marshy ground, did not seem to occur to anyone with the power to do anything about it. One of the bishops present at the battle (a number were killed) prophesied that Hungary would soon have twenty thousand new martyrs.

Although the arrangement was by now outdated by a century or two, the Hungarian order of battle on August 29, 1526, consisted of a vanguard and the right and left wing of the mainward, each of the three in a solid block of cavalry. Possibly because gunpowder weapons were viewed as unchivalrous, the few Hungarian cannon and harquebuses were positioned as the rearguard in purely defensive positions. After an initial volley, they played virtually no part in the battle.

So slipshod was the Hungarian plan of battle that even the crude Ottoman tactics were stunningly effective. The Turkish front rank consisted of the irregulars, volunteers, and conscripts that served as cannon fodder to blunt the force of an enemy's charge.

Behind the front rank, the Turks had placed their artillery, chained by the carriage wheels together in a single mass. Even if the Hungarians had captured the Turkish guns, this would have prevented them from turning the guns on the Ottoman main force, the janissaries with Süleymân personally in command. The janissaries were directly behind the artillery, with a hill at their back to anchor their line.

Louis opened the battle with a volley from the Hungarian guns, followed by a charge of the heavy cavalry. This easily smashed through the Turkish irregulars, leading the optimistic Hungarians to believe they had an easy victory. The rest of the army was ordered to advance.

The Hungarians had deceived themselves. Their heavy cavalry soon came up against the janissaries. There was a brief, if fierce, melee, with hand-to-hand fighting. At one point, even the sultan was hit with arrows and lances, although none penetrated his armor.

And perhaps nothing better illustrated the major Hungarian error: trying to fight a battle using swords, spears, and archery against a foe with firearms. The Hungarian knights were caught in crossfire as the Turkish artillery opened up and the janissary harquebusiers advanced, trapping the Hungarian cavalry between them.

Seeing their cavalry slaughtered, the Hungarian infantry began to withdraw. At that point, the *sipahis* charged the infantry, turning an orderly retreat into a rout.

It was over in less than ninety minutes. The Hungarians died by the thousands. Süleymân had ordered that there be no prisoners, and all who surrendered were executed. He did, however, shed a tear or two, probably sincere by his lights, over the body of Louis when it was found and identified.

John Zápolya and his army arrived the next day, but quickly retreated on hearing of the disaster. To this day, Hungarians remain divided on whether or not Zápolya was a traitor.

After ordering a massacre of all male peasants whom the Turks had conscripted (the women were kept as slaves), Süleymân advanced on Buda. He forbade looting but was completely ignored, and probably expected to be.

Entering the capital on September 10, Süleymân loaded everything of value he could into boats and burned the city. He spared only the royal palace, where he had taken up residence. He spent a while hunting and feasting, then built a bridge of boats across the Danube and passed through Pesth, burning the city to the ground.

It was simply not feasible to take possession of a country, even one gained so easily, at such a distance from Istanbul. Far better to treat the country as a special preserve to supply the Ottoman Empire with gold and slaves and as a steppingstone to Vienna, the taking of which was to remain Süleymân's unrealized dream his entire reign.

HISTORICAL NOTE: SÜLEYMÂN'S SHADOW

"Ibrahim the Magnificent"? Though beset by many trials
and tribulations, Ibrahim Pasha, the grand vizier known
variously as Pargah ("of Parga") or Maktul ("the Slain"),
managed to have a longer tenure than any other in that
extremely tenuous and dangerous position. Later grand
viziers habitually answered the sultan's summons with a
copy of their last will and testament in hand.

Born of Christian Greek parents in Parga, Ibrahim was
taken captive and enslaved by Turkish raiders as a young
boy. A widow in Magnesia purchased him, and she had
him educated and trained as a musician.

While still a teenager, he met and was purchased by
Süleymân, at that time heir-apparent to the throne of the
Ottoman Empire and governor of Magnesia. Impressed
with his new possession, Süleymân made him one of his
personal pages, then his chief advisor and favorite.

After Süleymân became sultan, Ibrahim was appointed
to a series of important positions in the palace. He became
Süleymân's constant companion, living in the imperial
suite, sharing meals and recreation, even keeping in constant communication through special messengers on the
rare occasions when they were apart.

This was not as odd as it sounds to modern ears. An
Ottoman sultan was probably one of the most isolated people on earth. It was very difficult for one to hear anything
even vaguely resembling the truth, especially given the
high mortality rate of those bringing bad news.

Added to this was Süleymân's extremely introverted per-
sonality, a natural development for someone raised in the

hothouse atmosphere of the harem. Relatives were one's most dangerous enemies. Süleymân needed someone like Ibrahim whom he could trust in order to keep some hold on sanity and to gain at least marginally objective opinions and feedback.

Ibrahim married the granddaughter of the man who had captured him in a grand ceremony. (The story that he married Süleymân's sister appears to be without foundation.) At a later feast in honor of the circumcision of five of the sultan's sons, Süleymân asked the grand vizier whether this celebration or his wedding was greater. Ibrahim, of course, answered that his own wedding had been more magnificent . . . for the guest of honor had been the sultan himself.

So rapid was his rise that even Ibrahim was worried. Cleverly, he joked with Süleymân not to raise him so high that he would be destroyed by his fall. Pleased with this reverse flattery, Süleymân swore an oath that Ibrahim would never be put to death as long as he himself held the throne.

Accounts of Ibrahim's fall vary. Most authorities attribute it to his effectiveness as a military commander in a war against the Persians and his awarding himself a title with the word *sultan* in it. But that was in the past. Arguments with another commander set in motion a chain of events that put him at odds with Süleymân. Intriguing on the part of Süleymân's queen, Sultana Hürrem, probably contributed to Süleymân's decision to have Ibrahim executed.

Since he had sworn not to kill Ibrahim, however, Süleymân sought legal counsel on how to obtain a release from his oath. The mufti he consulted issued a *fatwa* that permitted the sultan to break his word on condition that he build a mosque in Istanbul. Shortly afterward, Süleymân repented of what he now regarded as a rash act that deprived him of his best friend and counselor. For the rest of his reign in his poetry, he indirectly eulogized his friendship for Ibrahim.

4

VIENNA

1529

TURKEY in 1528 was the world's superpower, rivaled for that distinction only by the Spanish colonial empire that spanned the globe. The vast Ottoman Empire would reach its greatest extent under Süleymân I, "the Conqueror," known in Europe as "Süleymân the Magnificent."
   A bare two years previously, the sultan had invaded Hungary, the gateway to central Europe, and utterly destroyed the Hungarian army at the battle of Mohács. The young and impetuous King Louis II of Hungary had been killed on the field of battle, along with virtually every Hungarian who took part in the fight. Buda, the capital, had been occupied and then burned when Süleymân withdrew to Istanbul. His evacuation left a political and dynastic vacuum in what was left of Hungary.
   Politics as well as nature abhors a vacuum. Two rival claimants sought to fill the void left as a result of the havoc created by the Turks. The first of these was Archduke Ferdinand of Hapsburg. Ferdinand was the brother of Emperor Charles V. As brother-in-law of the childless King Louis, Ferdinand was considered to have a legal claim to the Magyar throne.

Ferdinand's rival claimant was John Zápolya, Prince of Transylvania. As a Hungarian, Zápolya could invoke the succession law of 1505 excluding foreigners from the throne of his country. With his army still fresh and intact in the field after his failure to join the muster of Hungarian nobility at Mohács, Zápolya was already in effective control of the greater part of the kingdom.

A Diet cobbled together by a faction of anti-German Hungarian nobles elected Zápolya king. He entered Buda with the air of a conqueror to be crowned. This suited Süleymân, who felt he could count on Zápolya to do his bidding.

In addition to Turkish acquiescence to his pretensions, Zápolya received material support from Francis I of France and his anti-Hapsburg allies. These were always willing to sacrifice the good of Europe as a whole for short-term gains to the advantage of France.

Countering Zápolya's usurpation, however, a rival Diet chose Ferdinand as king a few weeks later. Having already been elected king of Bohemia, and thus in a position of strength, a pro-German faction of the Hungarian nobility supported him.

This, as might be expected, led to a civil war in Hungary. Ferdinand engaged Zápolya in battle, defeated him, apparently with little effort, and drove him into exile in Poland. Ferdinand was then crowned king of Hungary.

Ferdinand occupied Buda and initiated moves to establish a central European Hapsburg state. This would be composed of Austria, Bohemia, and Hungary.

Such an arrangement would set up a strong imperial counter to the Polish-Lithuanian Commonwealth. It would

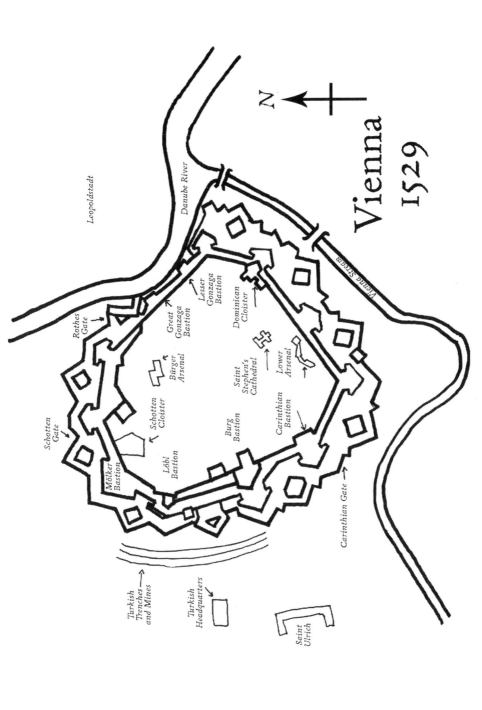

N

Vienna
1529

Leopoldstadt

Danube River

Vienna Stream

Rothes
Gate

Schotten
Gate

Mölker
Bastion

Löbl
Bastion

Schotten
Cloister

Bürger
Arsenal

Great
Gonzaga
Bastion

Lesser
Gonzaga
Bastion

Dominican
Cloister

Saint
Stephen's
Cathedral

Lower
Arsenal

Burg
Bastion

Carinthian
Bastion

Carinthian Gate

Turkish
Trenches
and Mines

Turkish
Headquarters

Saint
Ulrich

also pose a serious threat to further Turkish expansion into Europe. The Holy Roman Empire was not strong enough to drive the Turk from Europe completely. This was due to the rising tide of the Protestant Reformation, supported by France in the hope of weakening the empire.

Naturally, plans to establish a new political unit and contain the Turkish menace depended on the reaction of the Turks. In Turkish eyes, war was not the failure of diplomacy but its natural extension. With the rise of Süleymân the Magnificent, the Ottoman presence in Europe, both through diplomacy and warfare, was to have a profound effect on the course of European history.

Zápolya did not let matters rest with his defeat and exile. From his base in Poland, Zápolya sent an emissary to Istanbul. His goal was a military alliance with the sultan.

The envoy at first met with a distinctly chilly reception from Ibrahim Pasha, Süleymân's grand vizier, and his fellow viziers. This was clearly a bargaining tactic, however, as it was in Süleymân's interest to further Zápolya's ambitions.

Finally, having raised the anxiety level and put the Christian dog in his place, the sultan agreed to give Zápolya the title of king of Hungary. This would effectively grant the Transylvanian prince the lands that the sultan's armies had conquered in Hungary and make Zápolya, in essence, an Ottoman regional ruler, a "begler bey," but without requiring submission to Islam.

Süleymân promised Zápolya protection against Ferdinand and all his other enemies. A treaty was concluded in which Zápolya undertook to pay annual tribute to the sultan. A further provision placed a tenth part of the entire population of Hungary, male and female, at the disposal of the sultan every ten years. This meant that Süleymân could, as he wished, select up to 10 percent of the Hungarian people to enslave and deport to the auction blocks and harems of Istanbul.

In addition, Zápolya granted free passage through his territory to the Ottoman forces in perpetuity. John Zápolya thus became a vassal of the sultan.

Zápolya's portion of Hungary became nothing more than a puppet kingdom under Ottoman rule. It is not recorded whether the anti-German faction that elected Zápolya lived to regret having sold what was left of their country to the Turks.

In an effort to counter the activities of the pretender and secure a truce, Ferdinand sent his own embassy to Istanbul. His envoys, too, met with a chilly reception—only this one was genuine. Süleymân refused to consider any of the proposals and, in a fit of petulance, threw the ambassadors into prison.

Still, with Austria, Bohemia, and part of Hungary now united, the Turkish position was severely threatened. In early autumn of 1528, the sultan planned a new expedition to the north to counter the threat. This would be Süleymân the Conqueror's third campaign up the Danube Valley.

As "protector" of Zápolya against Ferdinand, and in defiance of Charles V (Ferdinand's liege lord), Süleymân aimed beyond Buda this time. His goal was the "Heart of

Europe," Vienna, the capital of the Holy Roman Empire.
As a German folk song put it,

> Hungary he'll soon depart,
> In Austria by dawn.
> Bavaria is next to fall,
> From there another land he'll take,
> And soon the Rhine he'll cross.

The situation could optimistically be described as desperate. . . .

THE SULTAN'S BREAKFAST

> To Sultan Süleymân the Magnificent, Commander of the Faithful, *etc.*
> Your breakfast is cold. You must be satisfied with what we can supply you from the guns on our walls.

That, more or less, was the gist of a message sent to Süleymân I during his siege of Vienna. The "Grand Turk" (as the Ottoman sultan was sometimes called in the West) had vowed to eat his breakfast amid the ruins of the city on the Feast of Saint Michael, now nearly a week and a half past. Still, Vienna showed no signs of giving in to Süleymân's demands in this cold and unseasonably wet October of 1529.

The campaign had officially begun May 10, 1529, when the horsetail standard led the Turkish armies, the largest ever assembled up to that time, out of Davut Pasa and headed north. Davut Pasa was the muster field outside Istanbul for all Ottoman military campaigns. While the sultan was in command, the actual prosecution of the campaign was left completely in the hands of Ibrahim Pasha, Süleymân's grand vizier.

Süleymân's first stop was Hungary, as he needed to secure a base from which to proceed to Vienna. Consequently, in early August, John Zápolya, accompanied by six thousand men, saluted his overlord on the field of Mohács. The combined Hungarian and Ottoman forces reached Buda by August 16, recapturing it after a brief siege.

After taking Buda, both Zápolya and Süleymân entered the city in triumph. The sultan received the pretender with great ceremony, placing the sacred crown of Saint Stephen on his head and naming him king of Hungary. Hungarian opponents of Hapsburg rule flocked to join the Ottoman host as it prepared to make its final approach on Vienna.

A month after the Turks reached Buda, the first parties of *akinjis*, the irregular cavalry units who provisioned and paid themselves by looting, crossed the Austrian frontier. They raided the province of Burgenland up to the walls of Vienna itself. The Viennese became almost used to the sight of a night sky made red with the flames of burning villages. Finally, the Turkish army moved out of Buda and advanced on Vienna in a body.

As had happened on their previous campaign three years before, the weather was appalling. The rains were heavier than ever before. The Danube was in flood, and the roads almost non-existent.

Many of the famous Turkish heavy siege guns, one of their greatest strengths, had to be left behind in Buda or were lost along the way, bogged down or sinking completely in mud. This created what proved to be a critical weakness in the Ottoman capacity to carry on an effective siege. The army advanced slowly, either forcing Hapsburg-held fortresses along the route into submission or bypassing them.

On September 27, a month later than originally planned, Süleymân the Magnificent pitched his camp before Vienna. By the end of the month, he had cut the city off from the outside world. Presently, as far as the eye could see around the walls of their city, the countryside was covered with the white blooms of thousands of Ottoman tents and pavilions, the most magnificent being, of course, that of Süleymân the Conqueror, easily visible from the city walls.

The city's defenses were not in the best of shape, nor were the number of defenders adequate to the task at hand. Ferdinand had encountered a great deal of difficulty in raising forces for the defense of Vienna.

Emperor Charles was fully occupied with a war in the west. To buy time, he counseled Ferdinand to undertake a truce with Zápolya. This would allow Charles to mount a major offensive once his own forces were free to engage on the eastern front.

Instead, Ferdinand carried out a personal recruiting campaign throughout his dominions. Everyone promised contingents, and in Austria, every tenth man eligible for military service was conscripted, whether or not his feudal dues had already been paid.

Ferdinand's action was not as impetuous as it might seem. It is hardly likely that either Zápolya or Süleymân would have agreed to a truce on any terms. Even if they had, they would have used the time to put themselves in a far more advantageous position than they already possessed.

Still, Ferdinand's efforts to gather sufficient resources were not enough. He also sought and received a measure of support from the imperial princes of Germany, addressing an appeal to the Diet of Speyer.

At first, they hesitated. The request might, after all, simply be a trick to raise an army to bring to book those who were flirting with Protestantism. The teachings of Doctor Martin Luther and others sounded very attractive both to rulers tired of seeing money flowing out of their realms to Rome and people divided in loyalty between a foreign Church and their own governments.

To counter these fears, Ferdinand put a great deal of emphasis on the boast recently made by Süleymân that he would not lay down his arms until he had erected a monument to his victory on the banks of the Rhine. This far from subtle reminder of the immediacy of the Turkish threat made some impression. Even Luther agreed to make an appeal for a stand against the Turks.

Luther's efforts turned out to be a trifle lukewarm, however. This was probably the result of his opinion that the pope was somehow the greater threat to Europe, or, at least, easier (and safer) to defy. Still, both Protestant and Catholic princes finally joined forces to vote a quota of troops for the defense of the empire.

Mobilization took time, however. Had Süleymân not been delayed a month due to the heavy rains, the imperial troops would not have been able to reach the city in time. As it was, the reinforcements arrived barely three days before Süleymân's main army encamped around Vienna.

As difficult as they had been to obtain, the imperial soldiers proved to be invaluable. The garrison was increased from twelve thousand to around twenty thousand. Even better, the troops were not the usual feudal levies palmed off to satisfy the obligation, composed of men "left over" from Charles's recruiting.

They were, instead, well-trained professional infantry, primarily the famous *Landsknechten*, or "country infantry." These were heavily armored foot soldiers that ruled the battlefields of Europe for two centuries or more. They were battle-hardened veterans, fresh from the emperor's campaigns in Italy.

The armored infantry had the added advantage of being under the command of Count Nicholas von Salm. Salm was a brave and experienced general with half a century of dedicated service in the imperial armies behind him.

There would be little chance that the Turks could rely on mistakes made by an impetuous and inexperienced commander as they had at Mohács. The presence of Salm was doubly fortunate, for Ferdinand was at Linz when the siege began, still attempting to raise forces for the defense of the city, and was not able to get back before the city was surrounded.

If the raising of reinforcements was providential, the repair and reconstruction of the city's defenses were a near-miracle. Vienna was half in ruins from the struggles of the previous century. The old medieval wall, barely six feet thick, surrounded the city. When finally demolished much later, the old wall would become the famous *Ringstraße*, or "Ring Street," circumscribing the financial and cultural center of Vienna. Outside the wall was a frail wooden palisade, pejoratively known to the inhabitants as "the City Hedge."

The condition of the defenses was a serious problem. The Ottomans were far more skilled at carrying out a siege than engaging in open battle. The armies of Süleymân the Magnificent had already successfully reduced Nándorfehérvár

(Belgrade) in 1521 and the island fortress of Rhodes held by the Knights of Saint John in 1522. Both had been far better defended than Vienna.

The sense of alarm within the city grew as pamphleteers began to publish stories of Ottoman atrocities, which, to be honest, scarcely needed exaggeration. They began comparing the impending siege to that of Constantinople over seventy-five years before.

The situations of Vienna in 1529 and that of Constantinople in 1453 were not, however, completely analogous. In taking Constantinople, Mehmet the Conqueror (the Turks were fond of that particular epithet) had attacked an isolated outpost in the heart of his own territory. Süleymân the Conqueror was operating in enemy territory at the edge of an extremely long line of communication and supply.

Mehmet, in addition, had obtained the services of a renegade artillery manufacturer, thus beginning the centuries of Turkish supremacy in gunnery. The Turks in 1453 had huge siege guns cast on the spot to pound the walls of the Queen City without cessation.

Süleymân had only light and medium guns at his disposal. These would have been inadequate against even the antiquated medieval wall of Vienna except after prolonged bombardment.

In anticipation of the siege, all the ground immediately outside the wall was cleared. Houses that had been built too close to the wall were razed.

Later it was decided that all buildings within artillery range had to be sacrificed to obviate any chance of the Turks using them for cover. This meant the destruction of the suburbs surrounding the city.

Approximately eight hundred buildings were burned to the ground. These included the city hospital, a number of churches and convents, and a castle built on a hilltop that could have served as a Turkish stronghold. Lacking the money and the time to build adequate stone bastions (strongpoints on the walls), earthen ramparts were thrown up around the city. Ironically, while employed as a fast and cheap expedient, earthen defenses were to prove superior to the more expensive stone walls. This was not the first time earthworks had been constructed. Historians believe, however, that it was due to their success during the siege of Vienna that their effectiveness was realized and their popularity caught on.

The earthen wall was twenty feet high. The system included a dry moat. Similar defenses were erected on the bank of the Danube. Entrenchments were dug inside the wall in case the Turks should manage to breach the walls and storm the city. Fire brigades were organized, and all roofs of flammable material were removed from the houses.

Stocks of provisions were laid in from a soon-depleted countryside, while non-combatants—old men, women, children, and priests—were evacuated. This was both for their own safety and to reduce the number of mouths to feed.

Vienna was now purely a military stronghold. Unfortunately, many of the evacuees fell into the hands of the wide-ranging *akinjis* and were killed or enslaved.

Finally, all but one of the city gates were bricked up. The sole exception, *Das Kärntner Tor*, the Carinthian Gate, was left open, which, along with a narrow sally port by the Hofburg Gate, would allow the defenders to make raids on the besiegers.

Having lost the advantage of heavy siege guns, Süleymân had to change tactics and rely primarily on mining; that is, digging tunnels from outside the city and setting off kegs of gunpowder that would bring the walls down. Before beginning hostilities, however, he called upon the garrison to surrender, claiming that his only goal was to find and punish the usurper Ferdinand.

This fooled no one, particularly since the sultan knew as well as the defenders that Ferdinand was not even in the city. If Süleymân's goal was as stated, the Austrian envoys suggested, there was no need for him to attack the city at all. His time would be better spent pursing Ferdinand in the field.

Süleymân further spoiled whatever effect his propaganda might have had by announcing that, if there was any resistance, he would be breakfasting in Vienna on the Feast of St. Michael the Archangel, a patron of the city, three days hence. He would level Vienna to the ground, leaving none of the population alive, and destroy the city so that future generations would doubt that it had ever existed.

The sultan's calculations might have been a little off. Lacking adequate siege engines, he could not breach the walls by cannonade and take the city by storm. The only event of note on St. Michael's Day, September 29, was a heavy rain. The level of misery in the light tents of the Ottoman army was high.

Two weeks later, there was still no improvement in the weather or the tactical situation. The defenders sent a released prisoner to Süleymân to inform him that his breakfast had grown cold. If he wanted something hot, he must be content to break his fast with what the defenders would willingly provide him from the guns on the city walls.

The siege now began in earnest. The defenders observed huge excavations that began in the distance, beyond artillery range. These earthworks soon became enormous and elaborate. Newly enslaved peasants dug trenches and mines, working without any protection. As the trenches came closer to the walls, these conscripts died by the thousands. They were expendable in Turkish eyes, however, and easily replaced by levies on subject populations. One observer noted that the defenders were tired of killing the slave engineers and that their harquebuses had become too hot to handle from continuous firing.

The killing was continuous as the conscripts slowly advanced their trenches through the rocky ground. This was due to the siege tactics usually employed by the Turks in contrast to those of European commanders. Where Europeans in general sought to preserve as many lives, productive assets, and as much infrastructure as possible for future use at as low a cost as possible, the Turks were after loot and conquest, regardless of the cost.

Thus, European sappers zigzagged their trenches when besieging a city or fort so that the defenders could not fire down on the workers. This took much longer, however, as more excavation was required.

The Ottomans placed speed above the toll in human lives and equipment. Their technique was to dig a series of broad, straight trenches directly toward the wall of a fortress.

The defenders could enfilade—fire directly down the length of this trench—at will. Sometimes the ground before the fortress could not be seen, obscured as it was by the countless bodies of the slaves thrown out of the trench by their fellows so that the work, driven by whips and threat of torture, might progress.

The Turkish advance drove inexorably forward: slow, bloody, and unbelievably costly. While slaves dug, guns pounded the walls and bastions of the city. On the average, more than one hundred shots a day were thrown at the city. This was a remarkable achievement considering the difficulty in hand-loading the artillery of the day.

Tactics changed as the network of trenches came closer to the wall. The conscripts were removed, and the final lines were built up more elaborately.

Buttresses and field fortifications were constructed parallel to the wall. This stopped the forward advance, but the digging continued.

A network of tunnels was pushed toward and below the walls. Skilled Turkish miners called *lagimjiyan* carried out this work as quietly as possible.

Above, the defenders dug countermines under the walls from inside the city in an attempt to preserve their defensive line. Inevitably some of these counterattacks were successful and Turkish tunnels were destroyed.

This was of no material importance. The Ottoman system relied on multiple assaults, with a large number of trenches and explosive charges.

The siege artillery that would rapidly have reduced the old walls to rubble had been lost forever in the marshes or left behind in Buda. Süleymân's assault on Vienna, therefore, depended completely on the success of these mining operations.

The theory was that at least some would succeed. At Rhodes, seven years earlier, for every mine intercepted and destroyed, several more reached their target. When the sappers laid their charges and exploded their mines, much of the city wall could crumble in an instant.

Christian traitors acting as spies inside the city, observing the strengthening of the fortifications, sent word to the sultan to inform him that the weakest point in the city's defense system was the section of wall on the southern side by the Carinthian Gate. The Turks concentrated their efforts in that quarter.

This does not mean that the defenders were otherwise left in peace to await the final assault. The marksmanship of the Turks was accurate and continual. This made it virtually impossible for any defender to appear on the wall without risking being hit.

Turkish archers, concealed among the ruins of the suburbs, let fly an incessant hail of arrows with deadly accuracy. Frequently, the arrows penetrated the loopholes and embrasures in the walls, making it dangerous for the citizens to walk the streets even in the normally safe area right under the walls.

Arrows were kept as souvenirs. Some, presumably discharged by Turks of distinction, were wrapped with costly fabrics and set with pearls.

Süleymân supervised operations from a carpeted pavilion, hung with fine tapestries and furnished with jeweled divans. The numerous pinnacles of the sultan's tent, crowned with knobs of gold, soared high above the Turkish encampment.

Here the sultan interviewed the Christian prisoners and sent them back into the city with threats and promises, laden with gifts of robes and Turkish ducats. This failed to have any effect on the defenders, who, in the words of a popular song of the day, appeared "not men, but devils" to the sultan.

Ibrahim Pasha, directing the siege, sought to encourage the attackers by distributing handfuls of gold in reward for an enemy's head or an important capture. This failed to have the desired effect. As the spirits of the besiegers flagged, *ceausi* had to drive them to the attack with clubs and whips.

The defenders did not sit idly by. Each day, a band of *Landsknechten* and a few support cavalry would mass inside the Carinthian Gate. The heavy doors would be unbarred, and they would rush out toward the enemy lines, pouring fire into the trenches and hacking away at the sappers.

One day they came back with thirty Turkish heads and ten prisoners. Another sally resulted in the capture of eighty prisoners and five camels. While material results from these forays were pitifully inadequate from the military point of view, the morale value of these charges was incalculable.

Still, the Turks, now regularly informed of conditions by their spies, had identified the most vulnerable sector of the defenses. They could direct the main assault accordingly.

The Viennese commanders could only watch with apprehension as the trenches close to the Carinthian Gate began to fill with the appurtenances of a major attack. These included ladders and fascines (bundles of wood) to pile up at the foot of the wall so that the barrier could be scaled.

Despite active countermining from the cellars of the city, breaches were made in the defenses when the Turkish sappers managed to explode some of their mines. The ensuing Turkish assaults were repulsed with difficulty.

Even though these attacks were clearly not the main assault, the Turks celebrated these relatively minor victories with the sound of trumpets and martial music. The defenders continued to make sorties of their own, sometimes returning with prisoners and loot.

When the unmistakable tall, conical caps with white neck-flaps of the janissaries began to predominate among the figures assembled below the walls, the defenders knew that the main assault would soon be coming, nor was it long delayed: Süleymân the Magnificent demanded quick results.

In the afternoon of October 9, a huge Turkish mine exploded near the Carinthian Gate. This created a gap approximately fifteen yards wide in the wall.

For some reason, however, the attack did not come immediately. This gave the Viennese a chance to rebuild the defenses slightly by piling rubble from the shattered wall into the breach. Finally, though, after a twenty-four-hour hiatus, the janissaries surged forward.

The Turkish army was, in its day, the most effective and efficiently organized military body in the world. Unfortunately, it was also bound in the iron grip of tradition. Novelty and innovation were far more likely to be punished than rewarded.

The price of this resistance to change was high at the siege of Vienna. The janissaries duplicated the tactic that had served Mehmet the Conqueror so well in the taking of Constantinople, massing all their forces for a single assault through the newly made breach in the wall. No effort was made to attack a number of points or even stage a diversion to draw off as many of the defenders as possible, spread thinly enough as they were.

Instead, the janissaries continued to attempt to force entry through the break near the Carinthian Gate. They ignored the fact that defensive technology had made great strides since the days of Mehmet the Conqueror.

The defenders had wisely massed their handguns and light cannon around the gap in the walls. When the janissaries charged into the breach, they were cut down by a devastating crossfire from the remaining portion of the wall and the earthworks. Janissaries fell by the hundreds, none of them managing to break into the city.

The next day, they launched another attack in the same place with identical results. On October 12, just before a third attack, another huge Turkish mine exploded.

This brought down most of the remaining wall, leaving a gap 150 feet wide. The attack that followed was beaten back in its turn.

Still, the defenders were in serious doubt as to their ability to hold out any longer. They did not know that the Turks were also in a difficult position.

On the evening of October 12, the sultan summoned a divan. This was a council of war to decide whether or not to continue the siege.

Ibrahim, voicing the views of the majority, favored withdrawal. Morale was low, winter was approaching, supplies were running short, the janissaries were grumbling, and the defenders expected reinforcements from Charles V at any moment.

Süleymân, however, decided on a fourth and final major assault. To maximize the possibility of success, he offered exceptional pecuniary rewards: The troops were each given a cash payment of one thousand asper (an asper being $^1/_{52}$ of a piastre), an amount roughly equivalent to twenty European gold ducats or forty silver thalers (dollars).

It was proclaimed throughout the camp that the first soldier to pass through the wall would receive thirty thousand asper, or about six hundred ducats, and immediate promotion. In an effort to rally his troops, the sultan himself came close to the walls to inspect the breach and then declared that the gap was large enough to make one final—and triumphant—assault.

On the morning of October 14, three massive columns surged toward the ruined defenses, to the accompaniment of weird (to European ears) music and the sultan's own banner to the fore. Officers with bared swords stood behind the troops to prevent any retreat.

After a halfhearted attack carried out in the face of a deadly crossfire from the defenders, however, the troops turned and ran. Some cried out that they would rather die at the hands of their own aghas than face the long Austrian harquebuses again.

The sultan ordered another mine exploded, after which the demoralized troops were to make one final attack. This, too, was thrust back.

Süleymân finally decided to end the attempt. Around midnight, the janissaries struck their tents and burned everything they could not carry away. Innumerable bonfires punctuated the darkness around the city.

By morning, the fires had died down and the vast Turkish host had decamped. The city awoke to a victory. The Viennese then discovered the charred corpses of captives who had been thrown into the flames. There were also the bodies of more than a thousand women and children, killed because they were not worth carrying into slavery, huddled in clusters with their throats cut.

The heart of Christian Europe was delivered from the Turk. Sultan Süleymân had suffered his first defeat, driven back from the walls of a great capital by a force that he outnumbered by at least three to one.

At Buda, his vassal, Zápolya, came out to complement him on his "successful campaign." It was as such that Süleymân endeavored to present it to his subjects on his return to Istanbul, celebrating his return with popular entertainments on the feast of the circumcision of his five sons in lavish and sumptuous style.

Süleymân tried to save face by pretending he had come not to take Vienna but to fight the Archduke Ferdinand. His success was demonstrated by the fact that Ferdinand had not dared to appear before him and was clearly no king but—in the subsequent words of Ibrahim Pasha—"only a little fellow of Vienna, and worth small attention."

HISTORICAL NOTE: DIRT CHEAP

The Holy Roman Empire in 1529 was not in the best financial condition. The Protestant Reformation was tearing *Mitteleuropa* apart, France was doing its usual best to undermine the power of both the empire and the Polish-Lithuanian Commonwealth, and the New World was still a serious drain on the imperial purse. As if to make certain that things were as bad as they could be, Süleymân the Magnificent was preparing to attack Vienna, the imperial capital and key to central Europe. The city's defenses were in terrible condition. The walls, especially, were in need of repair, to put it mildly. The antique structures were barely six feet thick, where they remained standing at all.

The city could not afford the extensive and expensive building program that would have been required to bring the walls up to snuff. In an effort to put together a defensive network, no matter how flimsy or ineffective, the citizens began throwing up a series of earthworks, huge ramparts surrounding the city, as well as embankments along the Danube.

Ironically, many historians credit this presumably inferior alternative with being the salvation of the city. Solid shot, ordinarily capable of eventually battering down even the strongest stone fortification, is completely ineffective against walls of earth. Instead of shattering the defenses, cannon balls tended to embed themselves in the soil, in some cases making the defenses even stronger.

It was also discovered that earthworks seemed to be largely immune to sapping. Ordinary stone walls, unless elaborate precautions were taken, could easily be undermined. A single mine could bring down an entire section of wall in a chain reaction.

Earthen ramparts, on the other hand, required much greater effort to sap and enormous quantities of powder to mine. Even then, the area affected by an explosion was relatively small. Much less damage was done at far greater cost to the attacker.

Repairs were easily carried out. Stone fortifications required some degree of skill to repair, especially in the heat of battle. Earthworks, however, could be designed and repaired by virtually anybody. All that was required was enough strength to dump dirt into the breach, with much of the material already at hand—even a massive explosion could not throw dirt very far. Soil is an extraordinarily good shock absorber.

There were, of course, disadvantages. An earthen rampart was far easier to scale than a stone wall. The amount of material that had to be dug, moved, and piled up was enormous. In order to achieve any kind of stability, the base had to be much broader than the top, which severely limited the height to which the defenses could be built.

The optimal combination seemed to be to have a strongpoint at the center of a defensive network, constructed with thick stone walls as high as possible, combined with concentric rings of earthworks. If a moat or two could be added to the mix, so much the better, particularly if it could be filled with water.

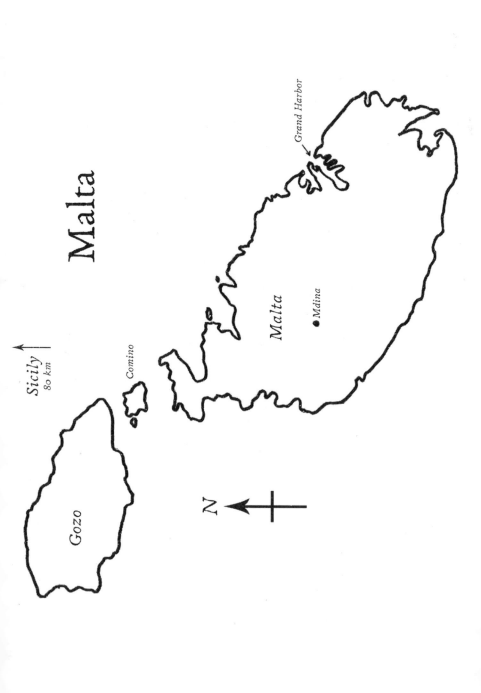

5

MALTA I

1565

SOME modern commentators wonder why Süleymân the Magnificent or Conqueror, known to Turkish posterity as "Süleymân the Just" or "Süleymân the Lawgiver," would even bother with a worthless piece of real estate like Malta in the first place. Today's pedant should ask Napoleon or Hitler the same question. One glance at a map of the Mediterranean will give the answer without too much thought. Lying just a few short leagues south of Sicily, Malta provides a logical stepping-stone to the conquest of the Italian peninsula.

With Malta under his control, the sultan could continue his attacks on central Europe from the east and take Christendom in a giant pincer movement, similar to that planned more than fifteen centuries earlier by Augustus Caesar. Süleymân should have remembered that Augustus stretched his resources too thinly across *his* empire and failed in the attempt as a result of the debacle in the Teutoburgerwald in AD 9.

From the beginning of his reign, Süleymân had dreamed of driving an invasion home into the heart of Europe. He had tried for Vienna, the key to *Mitteleuropa,* twice before, in 1529 and again in 1532. He succeeded in besieging it in

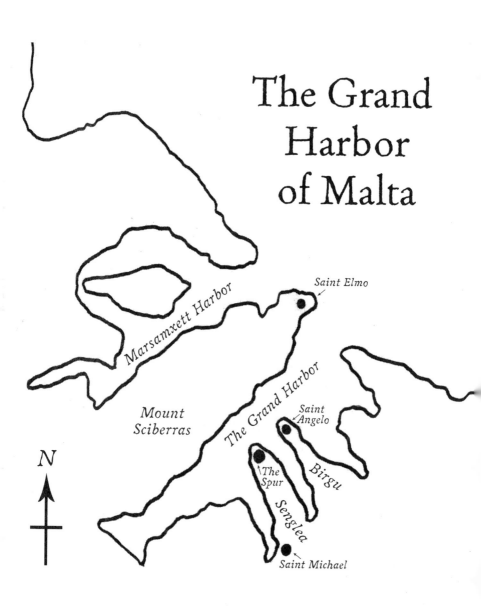

The Grand
Harbor
of Malta

Saint Elmo

Marsamxett Harbor

Mount
Sciberras

The Grand Harbor

Saint
Angelo

The
Spur

Birgu

N

Senglea

Saint Michael

1529 but had been driven back in humiliation after an epic defense. In 1532, he had not even managed to reach the city. Süleymân had inflicted disastrous defeats on the West a number of times, most notably at Mohács, the "Tomb of Hungary," in 1526. He had forced the withdrawal of the Knights of the Order, who now opposed him on Malta, from Rhodes in 1522. He had never, however, in common with his father and grandfather before him, managed to open a gateway into western Europe.

At first, Süleymân had planned on making yet one more assault on Vienna. Corsair-fashion, however, the ever-annoying Knights had made themselves and their activities too obtrusive to ignore any longer.

They had, of course, been raiding Ottoman shipping for years, costing the merchants of Istanbul immense sums of money. The straw that broke the camel's back, however, was their capture of a heavily laden merchantman in which Süleymân's harem had invested substantial amounts of their cash. Extremely valuable hostages had been taken, along with a cargo worth an estimated at eighty thousand ducats, over a third of a ton of gold.

With his eunuchs, wives, and concubines working on him, Süleymân allowed himself to be persuaded to try a campaign that targeted a European invasion from the south, rather than the east. He could then (at least in theory) make good that much earlier boast that he and his predecessors had made: to take Rome and stable their horses in Saint Peter's, turning the high altar into a feeding trough and the Blessed Sacrament into animal fodder.

As conquerors had known for centuries, the best route into Italy was through Sicily. The ancient breadbasket of the Roman Empire was both uniquely positioned for an invasion—the mainland is visible on clear days from the eastern point of the island—and particularly weak in its defenses.

To get to Sicily, however, meant Malta had to be taken— and that meant wiping out the Knights on Malta. The alternative was to leave a powerful and deadly foe in the rear, from which position it had already demonstrated its ability to make devastating inroads on Süleymân's plans for world conquest.

And that was a problem. . . .

SAINT ELMO'S FIRE

For two days, the tiny castle of Saint Elmo, an outmoded star fort named for the patron saint of seafarers, had suffered continuous bombardment and assault from the troops of Süleymân the Magnificent. Early on the morning of June 22, 1565, the Turks had opened the final attack on the little outpost with a bombardment so heavy it seemed as if the entire rockbound island of Malta shook under the impact.

The small fort had been completely hidden from sight in a cloud of dust and smoke. Obscured for hours under continuous shelling, observers on both sides were stunned finally to see the banner with the cross of Saint John, the emblem of the Knights of the Order, still flying above what was left of the battered walls of the fort when the haze finally cleared later in the day.

With this evidence of the survival of what remained of the garrison, Jean Parisot de la Valette, Grand Master of the Knights Hospitallers of the Order of Saint John of

Jerusalem, of Rhodes, and of Malta, had attempted to send reinforcements across the Grand Harbor from Castle Saint Angelo. They had been turned back.

As dawn broke over the island on the morning of June 23, the Turks began landing assault troops, positioning them around the base of the peninsula formed by Mount Sciberras where Saint Elmo's was perched, overlooking Bight Bay, Kalkara Creek, and Castle Saint Angelo to the south. The Turks, presumably because of superstitious fears, rarely launched night attacks.

At a signal, the guns on the Ottoman galleys opened up, joined by the giant siege weapons of the main batteries on land. When this bombardment ceased, the voices of the imams, Islamic prayer leaders, could be heard with their weird cries urging the faithful to attack and die for the Prophet, with the certainty of earthly honors and wealth if they conquered and lived or eternal ecstasy in the arms of countless beautiful *houris* if they died.

Barely a hundred defenders, many of them too weakened by wounds even to stand, opposed the thousands of assault troops. Two of the surviving Knights, the Sieur de Guaras and Sieur Miranda, had themselves taken to the breaches in the walls in carrying chairs and propped up so that they could continue to fight.

Even then, however, it took another hour before the massed attacks of the sultan's crack troops were able to overcome the last of the defenders. As the Turks poured into the crumbled and blood-soaked remains of Castle Saint Elmo, the last of the Knights dragged himself to the signal fire and lit it to inform the Grand Master that the enemy were within the walls.

It had taken nearly a month and cost tens of thousands of lives to take poorly fortified Saint Elmo. Only a few score Knights and men-at-arms had manned the outpost, many of them past what would ordinarily be considered the age of retirement.

Saint Elmo was a position that the sultan's engineers had estimated would take a few days at most and cost few men to overcome. As the Turkish army commander Mustapha Pasha and his staff toured the dripping, sanguinary ruins, he is reported to have gazed across the bay to the immense, heavily defended fortifications of Saint Angelo. Looking back to the wreckage that surrounded him, he is said to have exclaimed, "If so small a son has cost so dear, what price shall we have to pay for so large a father?"

Perhaps even more daunting was the fact that gaining the objective of Saint Elmo was, essentially, to have gained nothing and, ultimately, to have lost everything. There was no tactical or strategic advantage to occupying the little fort on the northern promontory, except that it gave the Turks access to an anchorage that they did not need.

The difficulties the Turks faced were not due to stupidity—or, at least, not completely. Had not the Knights made as much preparation as they could, they would not have been able to withstand so much as the first assault on the island, nor be in a position to capitalize on every mistake made by the all-but incompetent Ottoman commanders.

Trusting to their spy network, the Knights had known for some time that an attack was planned and that the target was Malta. This gave them some time to prepare, although it is doubtful that, given their relatively few resources compared to the invader, even the advance warning gave them much of an advantage.

La Valette, elected Grand Master in 1557 when he was sixty-three years old, was well aware of the caliber of his opponents. He had been a galley slave of the Turks for a year until ransomed by his brother Knights.

The Grand Master set to work immediately with the limited resources of the Order to beef up the island's defenses. First, he strengthened Castle Saint Elmo by adding to the walls and throwing a ravelin, a *v*-shaped earthwork outside the main ditch covering the area between two bastions, across the southern approach.

There was so little earth and brush on Malta available for this project that sticks and dirt had to be imported from Sicily. The more costly and time-consuming alternative would have been to cut a moat out of living rock. Even so, the work was barely completed when the Turkish invasion came.

La Valette sent word to all members of the Order throughout Europe to hasten to the defense of the only territory remaining to the Knights. Taking advantage of the barrenness of the island, the Grand Master ordered all sources of water outside the defenses poisoned and all crops gathered in. Any invasion force would have to bring everything with it or die of thirst and starvation.

In no mood to trust the promises of the Turk, the Maltese sought refuge behind the defenses of the Order. They had previous experience of the Ottoman threat as the result of a raid on the tiny northern islet of Gozo some years before. Nearly all the inhabitants had been carried off into slavery.

Malta was nominally under the suzerainty of Philip II of Spain. La Valette, therefore, first attempted to obtain reinforcements from that source. Don Garcia de Toledo, the Spanish viceroy of Sicily, made some promises. In light of the fact that he was responsible for the defense of Sicily, however, and was himself not receiving requested reinforcements, he could do little else than make promises he was probably fully aware he would not be able to keep.

There were good reasons for this lack of assistance. Philip, far from the monster depicted in modern fiction, had to deal with unrest on the part of recently converted Muslims in his kingdoms. These were preparing to rise in support of any successful Turkish action.

Had Philip stripped his garrisons of men to reinforce either Malta or Sicily, his own depleted defenses would have been attacked immediately. The anticipated "Morisco Revolt" did, in fact, come less than five years later. This was on the occasion of Süleymân's son and successor, Selim the Drunk, beginning his own program of conquest by breaking a peace treaty with Venice and invading Cyprus.

La Valette had a little over five hundred Knights and men-at-arms to man his defenses at the beginning of the siege. These he distributed as equitably as he could among the three main strongpoints, Castle Saint Angelo at Birgu, Castle Saint Michael at Senglea, and Castle Saint Elmo out on the northern peninsula that embraced the Grand Harbor. The capital of Mdina with its ramshackle defenses in the center of the island was evacuated except for a force of cavalry.

The members of the Order were supported by approximately one thousand Spanish infantry and between three to four thousand irregular Maltese militia and volunteers. These, in turn, were supplemented by bands of guerrilla fighters made up of townsmen and peasants. Without their help, the island had no hope whatsoever of resisting the coming assault. This brought the estimated total strength of the defenders up to a maximum of approximately sixty-five hundred or seven thousand men.

Opposing them were the finest soldiers of the Ottoman Empire. Süleymân the Magnificent well knew the timber of the men he faced and was not the sort to do things by halves.

The sultan scoured his immense domain for the best of everything, especially fighting men, and scraped together every available ship for transport and supply. This was a particular necessity, for nearby Tunis and Tripoli could not provide sufficient fodder for man or beast, and virtually everything would have to be hauled the endless leagues between Istanbul and the barren rock of Malta.

The number of effectives with which Süleymân prepared to invade Malta is estimated at between thirty and forty thousand men. Most of these consisted of the famed janissaries, the "New Soldiers" with their white robes and high peaked hats decorated with heron plumes, and *sipahis*, feudal levies of cavalry.

Supplementing the regular troops were approximately four thousand *jayalars*. These were dervishes who actively sought death in battle and were used as front line shock troops. There were also some irregular volunteers who served in order to plunder.

Accompanying the fighting force were the slave engineers and sappers so necessary to the costly siege methods of the Turks, as well as other support personnel. These usually outnumbered combatants by a factor of 1½, so the total number of men assembled by Süleymân was probably in excess of one hundred thousand, counting sailors and non-combatants.

This was smaller than the expeditionary force the Turks usually fielded, but, consisting as it did of the very finest the Ottoman Empire had to offer, would presumably be multiplied many times over in effectiveness. The relatively smaller size would also make resupply somewhat easier by reducing the quantity of goods that had to be shipped.

A fleet of more than two hundred vessels carried the Ottoman force, to which were added a large number of ships provided by private investors. War was a business to the Turks, and one on which the prosperity of the entire empire depended.

This aggregated might of the Ottoman Empire was to be thrown headlong against an island of barely 150 square kilometers with few defenders and largely makeshift fortifications.

The Ottoman Empire was one of the few large political entities not only to survive but to grow rich on piracy and plunder, at least for a time. When it finally went into a decline, it was through lack of new external conquests combined with internal rot.

Except for war and terror, the Ottoman Empire is not remembered for producing anything, but for converting the loot of other civilizations to its own use. A case in point was the greatest religious edifice in the empire, the Hagia Sophia, the Church of the Divine Wisdom, formerly used as a mosque and now a museum.

The Hagia Sophia was the principal shrine of Orthodox Christianity before the capture of Constantinople in 1453. Even the famed Blue Mosque is a direct copy of Byzantine elements constructed by renegade Christian engineers and slave labor.

Command of the Ottoman task force was split, with no supreme commander. While this might have seemed like a good idea at the time, it was to have fatal consequences.

Overall command of the army was given to Mustapha Pasha; *pasha* is generic for either "general" or "admiral." That of the navy was assigned to Piali Pasha, married to a granddaughter of the sultan.

Mustapha had failed once already against the Knights, although redeeming himself in subsequent campaigns against Muslim rebels. Piali, the sultan's grandson-in-law, had taken the island of Djerba to the south of Malta from the Spanish.

Among other notables in the initial invasion force, Mustapha and Piali were to be joined later by Torghoud Rais, better known in the West as "Dragut." Torghoud Rais was considered the greatest seaman, Christian or Muslim, of his day. It was he who had raided Gozo fourteen years earlier and carried off the people to slavery after reconnoitering Malta for any weak points.

Lookouts of Saint Elmo and Saint Angelo sighted the masts of the Turkish fleet on Friday, May 18, 1565. La Valette immediately sent four of the Order's galleys out under the command of Chevalier de Romégas to reconnoiter.

La Valette also sent a small boat north to Sicily informing de Toledo that the siege had begun and requesting reinforcements. De Romégas was the Order's admiral of the galleys and quite possibly nearly the equal of Torghoud Rais in seamanship.

It seemed at first that the Turks were heading for South Wind Harbor, "Marsasirocco." They bypassed this, however, and went on to anchor in a small bay near the village of Mgarr on the northwest coast of the island.

The invaders were probably searching for a better anchorage on the west from which they could launch an attack on the fortified positions in the eastern part of Malta. This would allow them to not only devastate the entire island but also secure a port as far from the defenders as possible to prevent sorties from destroying their irreplaceable supplies.

Almost immediately, an argument began among the Turkish commanders over the best place to establish a base. After wasting half a day, the decision was made to use Marsasirocco after all, and the fleet moved to that location.

Marsasirocco should have been adequate as a staging area for the entire campaign. It was sheltered from all winds but those from the south (hence its name), and even those were rare in summer, the campaigning season. It was also a singularly healthy location, being far removed from the swamp that resulted from inadequate drainage (Malta is practically a solid outcropping of limestone) closer to the position of the Knights.

Some of the pashas, however, wanted a harbor that was sheltered in all directions in all weather. That meant either the Grand Harbor, around which was grouped nearly all the strength of the Knights and their allies, or Marsamuscetto, separated from the Grand Harbor by the peninsula of Mount Sciberras and guarded only by the guns of little Saint Elmo. These anchorages thereby became a prime—if completely unnecessary—objective of the campaign.

Lacking manpower, the Knights and the Maltese were unable to counter the Turkish landing by "catching them with their feet wet." The Ottoman force landed without opposition and the commanders began considering their next step.

The Turks soon made their second mistake. Instead of attacking weakly defended Mdina, they chose to concentrate their first effort on the Post of Castile, a small strongpoint on Birgu, just south of Castle Saint Angelo.

As a result, throughout the siege, la Valette was able to send messengers through Mdina, up to Gozo, and from Gozo by boat to Syracuse, less than twenty-five leagues away. Mdina also had the best sources of water and the most fertile land on the entire island, both items of immense value to the Turks if only they had taken advantage of them.

Instead, the invaders picked the Post of Castile, choosing it on the strength of a confession wrung from a captured Knight, Adrien de la Rivière of the French Langue. Under torture, he gave out the information that if Mustapha wanted a quick victory, he should attack the weak and poorly defended Post of Castile.

Mustapha immediately ordered an attack, lost hundreds of his best troops, and had de la Rivière beaten to death for lying—which is precisely what he had done. The Post of Castile turned out to be not the weakest point in the defenses but the strongest. Mustapha called off the attack, retreated, and summoned a council to try and decide what to do next.

The militarily obvious thing to do would have been to occupy the Corradino Heights, to the south of low-lying Birgu and Senglea, and Mount Saint Margherita, on the stumpy little peninsula north of Kalkara Creek and northeast of Castle Saint Angelo. Securing these positions would have given the Turks the ability to sweep the strongest defenses of the Order with unopposed artillery fire for as long as they wished at virtually no danger to themselves.

It would also bottle up the Knights and their allies, confining them to the few small town lands they occupied. This was because the Ottoman galleys had already sealed off the Grand Harbor.

Instead, Pasha-Admiral Piali and Pasha-General Mustapha got into an argument. Mustapha Pasha wanted a land triumph due solely to himself that he could report to the sultan. Said triumph, however, would require the assistance of the navy to move troops effectively, thus putting the vessels and sailors in range of the defenders' shore batteries. Piali Pasha, on the other hand, wanted to protect the immense fleet that Süleymân had entrusted to his care.

The Grand Harbor was clearly out of the question. Although Marsasirocco was more than adequate for his purposes, Piali Pasha apparently was not familiar with conditions in the central Mediterranean. He expected sudden and drastic changes of weather.

This meant Marsamuscetto, the inlet just north of Mount Sciberras, was the only choice, sheltered as it was in all directions. It was also directly under the guns of Castle Saint Elmo.

Mustapha was an old campaigner of moderate ability who had the ear of the sultan. Piali was a young naval commander who was the sultan's grandson-in-law and had direct access to the most influential inhabitants of the harem. Piali won the argument.

Mustapha now sent engineers in to assess the situation of Saint Elmo. It turned out to be an old-fashioned and relatively simple arrangement, similar to many that the Turks had overcome countless times before with little effort.

Saint Elmo was a "star" fort with four main salients or outcroppings. The front, where the main attack would be concentrated, was broken into a bastion, a strongpoint on the walls. A cavalier (a defensive work, usually *v*-shaped like a ravelin but within the main fortification and standing higher than the main ramparts) protected the fort on the seaward side and was separated from Saint Elmo proper by a ditch.

Landward, the defenses were buttressed with a counterscarp, the outer side of a defensive ditch, and the small ravelin already noted. The cavalier was connected to the castle by a drawbridge, while the ravelin had a fixed bridge.

It all appeared simple and straightforward. Mustapha decided to attack.

Had the Ottoman general made that decision in the beginning, things might have turned out differently. As it was, he had to shift his entire army and the massive siege equipment the whole way around the circumference of the Grand Harbor.

Mustapha also had to abandon the siege works already started around Birgu and begin anew in front of Saint Elmo—after hauling the necessary materials from the south of the island and over the rocky wasteland, for there was neither soil nor brush on Mount Sciberras peninsula. A week was wasted making the switch.

La Valette used the respite to good advantage. He put every available body—man, woman, and child, soldier and citizen, slave and free—to work strengthening the defenses of Saint Angelo and the surrounding fortified townships. He manufactured gunpowder, prepared Greek firebombs, hauled cannon balls, dug trenches, and repositioned guns.

La Valette was fully aware that Castle Saint Elmo could not survive. He could, however, make the taking of it costly in men, munitions, and, most especially, time. If the tiny fort, now the key to the entire island, could hold out for any length of time, the chances of the defenders could be increased dramatically.

Seeking to encircle Saint Elmo, Mustapha had entrenchments dug in the solid rock of the island. He ruthlessly sacrificed the lives of his conscript engineers and sappers, as was the Turkish practice.

By the end of May, Mustapha had begun the bombardment of Saint Elmo, his gunners methodically alternating cannon balls of iron, stone, and marble. The iron balls were for battering at long range, the heavier stone projectiles for more effect closer in, while marble balls shattered into shrapnel. It was not long before portions of Saint Elmo's landward defenses began to crumble.

Late one night, a delegation from Saint Elmo slipped across the Grand Harbor to Saint Angelo. Realizing that their situation was hopeless, a number of the younger Knights requested permission to abandon their station.

La Valette shamed them into going back by declaring that he would himself go with a picked band and take up their posts. In any event, each night, fresh troops were ferried across, and the sick and wounded removed to the Great Hospital of the Order in Birgu, possibly the finest medical facility in the world at the time.

Bombardment of Saint Elmo was continuous. It must have seemed miraculous that such a small fort with its miniscule garrison could hold out for so long.

Finally, however, the great Torghoud Rais arrived. He brought personal word from Süleymân that the two quarreling Ottoman commanders were to defer to his advice in everything. This effectively placed Torghoud Rais in the position of supreme commander.

Torghoud Rais took in the situation at a glance. Exhibiting enormous contempt for the two harem favorites who had so far royally fouled up the siege, he subjected them to a highly skilled and colorful tongue-lashing.

The new commander informed Mustapha and Piali of every mistake they had made, and probably more besides, employing the imaginative invective that seems to come naturally to speakers of Arabic, likely adding a series of comments regarding their ancestry and dietary habits. He pointed out the obvious fact that they should have taken the north of the island first, securing a base from which the rest of Malta could be reduced by concentrating on the strongpoints of Birgu and Senglea. Saint Elmo should have been completely ignored.

Having committed so much to taking the little fort, however, Torghoud Rais rightly felt that he had no choice but to continue the attack. Breaking off the engagement would have been devastating to troop morale, to say nothing of looking like a retreat—and the Turks did not engage in strategic retreats.

Within a matter of days, the counterscarp and ravelin were in Turkish hands and numerous breaches opened up in the walls. Torghoud Rais's assessment was that it would not be long before the breaches were wide enough for a massed assault in traditional Turkish fashion.

Torghoud Rais had, of course, taken great pains to bring this about. The new Ottoman commander-in-chief repositioned the heavy siege guns for a devastating crossfire for maximum effect.

More importantly, Torghoud Rais realized almost instantly that Saint Elmo's strength was being renewed nightly from Saint Angelo. He immediately ordered Piali Pasha to patrol the Grand Harbor after dark, cutting off the reinforcements at the source. Even so, the fort that Torghoud Rais had expected to fall in a few days held out for three more weeks.

On June 21, the Order celebrated the Feast of Corpus Christi ("the Body of Christ") in traditional fashion. All available Knights and civilian dignitaries marched in procession in full ceremonial dress behind a monstrance (a special holder, usually of precious metal) containing the Blessed Sacrament. The special prayer offered during the ceremony was that their brethren in Saint Elmo would not "perish utterly by the merciless sword of the Infidel."

The next day, the final assault began, and the day after that, the fort finally fell. Castle Saint Elmo, expected to collapse within a few days, had held out for thirty-one. Among those who died during the attack was Torghoud Rais, like Wolfe at Quebec, living long enough to know that Saint

Elmo had been taken and "dying happy." Other casualties included a number of important pashas, the agha or leader of the janissaries, and the Turkish master gunner, a key individual in any siege operation.

Against Mustapha's direct orders, some few of the Knights in Saint Elmo had survived. In a disgusting, albeit typical, display of contempt for Christianity and the Knights, Mustapha had the survivors decapitated and their bodies nailed to crosses. These he launched across the Grand Harbor directly across from Castle Saint Angelo. Four of these washed up the next day on the rock shelf below the fort.

What la Valette then did is understandable but hardly excusable from a Christian perspective in this writer's view, particularly as he already knew the enemy he was fighting and what he could have expected of him—the Turks rarely gave quarter and took few prisoners from among those who resisted their attacks. He emptied the dungeons of Saint Angelo of all Turkish prisoners, cut off their heads, and fired the grisly projectiles from his guns at their erstwhile comrades in arms across the bay.

From that point on, one Turkish prisoner was hanged each day from the ramparts of Mdina. Clearly this was to be a fight to the finish, with no quarter given or asked on either side.

HISTORICAL NOTE: PEREGRINI

Today everyone knows the Order of the Holy Religion (an informal name for the Knights) as "the Knights of Malta." From their rather lengthy full name, the Knights Hospitallers of the Order of Saint John of Jerusalem, of Rhodes, and of Malta, however, it is plain that they must have had other homes. How did they end up on the three rocky little islands south of Sicily?

After the loss of Rhodes in 1522, for which the Knights had put up such stiff resistance as to wrest favorable terms from the normally intractable Süleymân the Magnificent, the Order was without a home. It took up temporary residence in Viterbo, north of Rome, and then in Nice, France.

No ruler, however, particularly wanted a potential loose cannon in his dominions in the form of a sovereign and independent order of knighthood. Vivid memories still remained of the Templars, who had to be suppressed, and the Teutonic Knights, the Grand Masters of which had become rulers of the *Ordenstaat* that straddled Prussia and Poland and who eventually apostasized and set themselves up as the House of Brandenburg, ancestors of the German kaisers.

Wanderers for eight years, the Knights saw an opportunity open up when Charles V was elected Holy Roman emperor in 1530. Part of his enormous patrimony consisted of the Maltese archipelago.

While occupation of the islands had been suggested previously on a number of occasions, it had been rejected because of the barren condition and the tiny size. Besides, the Order expected any day to mount an offensive to retake their real home, Rhodes, back from the infidel.

Still, the island had one advantage rare in the Mediterranean. It had not one, but two first class harbors, not to mention a number of others superior to almost everything else around.

That settled the matter. The Knights had come to view the military aspect of their vocation as being primarily connected with the sea. A delegation was sent from the Order to the new emperor, and a petition entered for possession of the barren rocks.

After some deliberation, the emperor agreed and handed over Malta to the Knights in return for an annual nominal tribute of one falcon. (Remember Dashiell Hammet's novel and the Humphrey Bogart film based on it?) Charles added a rider to the grant. The Knights would have to garrison the city of Tripoli, recently taken, and maintain it as a base for launching a possible future Crusade.

The Knights settled in to make the best of what many regarded as a temporary home, a stepping stone to the recovery of Rhodes. They built fortifications, facilities for their galleys, and, most important in many respects, the Great Hospital.

Alone of all the Hospitallers, the Knights of the Order of Saint John still maintained superb medical facilities. Contrary to the usual myth about the state of medieval European medicine, the medical Knights were probably the best physicians in the world. Even the military Knights put effective hygiene measures in place on campaign, an almost unheard-of precaution.

By the Rule of the Order, all patients were treated "as if each were Christ Himself." This they did whether the patient was Catholic, Protestant, Jew, or Muslim, although to avoid inadvertent infringement of the various dietary restrictions or ritual contamination, each were maintained in separate wards. The Knights themselves served patients of whatever faith off plates of gold and silver.

The Order remained on Malta until 1798, by which time their loss of mission against the Turk had led to a certain degeneracy and growing animosity on the part of the native population. Napoleon easily ousted them, and they were again homeless.

An interesting side note is that the wandering Order petitioned the new United States government sometime around 1805 for some land in the American west to build a new home and bring civilization to the area. The United States turned them down, maintaining that harboring an aristocratic and autonomous mini-state was inconsistent with the republican form of government.

The last sovereign order of knighthood in the world (the revived and reformed Teutonic Knights are no longer sovereign, having lost the last of their temporal possessions in 1805), the territory of the Order is confined to a few buildings in downtown Rome and various hospitals and other facilities that they maintain throughout the world. While the organizational structure is still military, the Knights now confine themselves and their membership to acts of charity and humanitarian aid.

6

MALTA II

1565

ANTICIPATING an easy victory, the Ottoman sultan Süleymân the Magnificent had ordered an attack on the tiny island of Malta, a rocky bit of nothing a few leagues south of Sicily that could provide a steppingstone for the conquest of Europe. As an added inducement, Malta was the home of the Knights of the Order of Saint John of Jerusalem, of Rhodes, and of Malta, a sovereign military religious order owing fealty directly to the pope and the most dangerous adversaries faced by the Turks in their quest to conquer the world.

Unfortunately, the invasion under the joint command of Mustapha Pasha and Piali Pasha had been badly bungled. Instead of directing efforts toward conquest of the northern half of the island and the subsequent reduction of the two strongpoints of Birgu and Senglea, they had attempted to secure an unnecessary anchorage north of the Mount Sciberras peninsula by reducing the otherwise unimportant and tiny Castle Saint Elmo.

Expected to fall within two or three days at most, the assault on Saint Elmo had dragged on for weeks. It was only with the timely arrival of Torghoud Rais, a brilliant Ottoman naval commander who took charge of operations, that the little fort finally fell after a siege of thirty-one days.

Torghoud Rais was killed in the final attack, along with thousands of others, against a garrison that numbered by then less than a hundred effectives. The two rival commanders, Piali Pasha and Mustapha Pasha, were again left in charge of the invasion, and immediately set to work further bungling the operation. . . .

SAINT ELMO'S PAY

With the fall of Castle Saint Elmo and the death of Torghoud Rais, Mustapha Pasha began the lengthy process of shifting operations from Mount Sciberras peninsula back to his former position in front of Senglea and Birgu, a hellish task under existing conditions. This involved transporting not only the ordinary impedimenta of a besieging army but the fortifications themselves, Malta being too barren to provide any raw materials on the spot.

Jean Parisot de la Valette, Grand Master of the Order, now received some extraordinary news. On June 23, 1565, the very day that Saint Elmo fell and, coincidentally, or providentially depending upon your perspective, the eve of the Feast of the Birth of Saint John the Baptist, the Patron Saint of the Order, a small relief force from Sicily had landed on Gozo, a little islet off the north coast of Malta.

Among the relief force were forty-two Knights who had not been able to reach Malta before the siege, a number of "gentleman volunteers" from all over Europe including two Protestant enthusiasts from England, fifty-six gunners, and approximately six hundred Spanish infantry. Don Juan of Austria, bastard half-brother of King Philip II of Spain, had tried to sneak away and join the expedition as well, but had been caught.

Remarkably, there were also two young Jews. Their ancestors in the faith—if not direct blood ancestors—had been expelled from Spain nearly three quarters of a century before and from England and France even earlier. They, however, had decided that Christian bigotry was infinitely preferable to the horrors of life under the Turks.

The presumed haven for Jews to be found in Islamic countries had proved to be ephemeral, although there were some exceptions. Those who survived torture and imprisonment by the Muslims made their way to northern or central Europe or accepted conversion to Christianity and returned to Spain.

On the night of June 29, the Sieur de Robles, the brother Knight in command of this rather variegated relief force, brought his men completely unscathed through enemy lines to Saint Angelo, guided by Maltese peasants who knew every hidden path and byway. The Turks only learned about the reinforcements the next morning when the ringing of bells and the incongruous sound of laughter and shouting from the battlements alerted them to what had happened.

Mustapha became disheartened by the arrival of fresh troops. Unwilling to undertake a new assault without the assistance of his miracle worker Torghoud Rais, he offered terms to la Valette. These were safe passage for the Order and their supporters with full honors of war; that is, they would be able to retain personal weapons and selected artillery.

Having no reason to trust the word of a Turk, la Valette led the emissary blindfolded to a point in the middle of the defenses. Removing the blindfold, he directed the man's eyes to the height of the walls above and the depth of the ditch below.

The Grand Master then gave his reply to Mustapha's terms by informing the messenger that the ditch before the castle was the only territory he would give Mustapha . . . on condition that he fill it with the bodies of his janissaries.

Mustapha now shifted into high gear. He finally occupied the Corradino Heights to the south of Castle Saint Angelo as well as Mount Saint Margherita to the northeast. He then secured the Grand Harbor by dragging a small fleet of galleys into the Marsa, the lower portion of the Grand Harbor, across the spit of land that separated it from the northern inlet of Marsamuscetto, thus avoiding the guns of Saint Angelo.

The Knights could not use their own galleys, laid up in the sea moat between Birgu and Senglea, for Turkish guns now commanded the entire Grand Harbor except for a small space in front of Castle Saint Angelo. The defenders were now completely bottled up, although individual messengers could still slip out and make their way to Gozo by way of Mdina and thence to Syracuse, keeping the rest of Europe informed of the progress of the siege.

By the first week of July, Mustapha had finally made what he considered adequate preparations. The batteries on the Corradino Heights and Mount Saint Margherita opened up with crossfire on the fortifications of Senglea and Castle Saint Angelo. Mustapha's plan was first to soften up the landward defenses and then make a simultaneous land and sea assault on the Senglea peninsula.

What Mustapha did not know was that the defenders had somehow divined his plan and had prepared well for it. The Maltese militia, all of whom were expert swimmers, had erected an underwater palisade and series of obstacles along the only portion of the Senglea peninsula suitable for carrying out a landing.

On July 15, Mustapha launched a massive attack by land across the Senglea peninsula and by sea across the Grand Harbor from Marsa. There were three separate parts to the attack.

The main thrust was by water, straight into the hidden defenses prepared by the Maltese. The secondary attack was a frontal assault on the landward defenses.

Seemingly completely suicidal, there was, nevertheless, a method in Mustapha's madness. A third force, consisting of nearly a thousand picked janissaries, was loaded into ten boats at the foot of Mount Scibarras and slipped across the Grand Harbor to Dockyard Creek on the northeastern side of the Senglea peninsula, from which the defenders had been drawn by the attack on the landward defenses.

The main sea attack came to almost immediate grief. The boats either ran against the hidden stakes of the underwater palisade and were holed or got hung up on the chains laid between the stakes. The gunners and harquebusiers on shore subjected the stranded Turks to murderous fire.

Meanwhile, the Maltese militia swam underwater to counter any Turkish effort to free the boats. They engaged in a furious submarine hand-to-hand battle which churned the water red with blood—mostly Turkish. One professional soldier remarked later that he had never seen courage to equal it by the men of any nation.

It soon became obvious that the main assault by sea was a failure. As the boats pulled away (those that could, anyway), a number of Turks were left behind. Many of the abandoned Turks attempted to surrender, but the Maltese had too vivid a memory of what these same men had done to the few survivors of Castle Saint Elmo barely a week before. They seized the Turks and cut their throats, calling out "Saint Elmo's pay!" as they did so. They then looted the bodies of their silken robes, jeweled scimitars, and turbans and threw the corpses into the water, where they remained bobbing about for days.

The landward assault was slightly more successful. The fortuitous circumstance—for the Turks—of the explosion of a powder magazine opened up a sizable breach in the wall. Some of the attackers managed to achieve a toehold on the wall itself.

Despite these advances, this portion of the attack was not meant to be anything more than a holding action until the sea assault should have its effect. The most dangerous part of the attack, however, proved to be the janissaries who had been slipped across the Grand Harbor to take Senglea in the rear from the northeast.

This force passed between the tips of the headlands of Senglea and Birgu unobserved . . . or so they thought. The low walls on this side of the peninsula were virtually abandoned and wide-open to attack.

What the janissaries did not know was that there was a masked battery at the foot of Castle Saint Angelo right at the water's edge on the shore of Birgu. It had been placed there for just such a contingency.

Sieur de Guiral of the French Langue was in command of the battery. He could hardly believe his eyes when he saw ten boatloads of janissaries in their distinctive uniforms come floating down Dockyard Creek practically at point-blank range.

De Guiral waited until all ten boats were directly in front of his guns and then gave the order to open fire. It was, to coin a phrase, like shooting fish in a barrel.

Only one of the boats managed to escape, limping back across the Grand Harbor. The others were sunk almost immediately, their occupants either drowned or torn to pieces by the fire from the guns.

At least eight hundred, possibly more, of Süleymân's finest soldiers had died in a matter of minutes without being able to strike a blow. Had they been able to land, Senglea would have fallen almost as rapidly as the attackers themselves were wiped out. Mustapha Pasha retired from the fray to come up with another plan.

Obviously the infamous Turkish tactic of throwing more and more men into the fight and overwhelming the opposition by sheer numbers was not going to work. Within days, the Ottoman general had decided once again to split the command between himself and Piali Pasha.

Mustapha would take care of Senglea while Piali targeted Birgu. With a roar that could be heard in Sicily and Italy, the bombardment opened at dawn on August 2, with every gun the Turks had concentrated on these two objectives, and continued for hours.

Finally a trumpet call signaled the end of the barrage. Before the guns had finished firing, thousands of janissaries charged down from the heights that looked down on Senglea and Birgu. In an attack lasting six hours, the Turks threw themselves again and again at the walls, on several occasions even managing to attain positions in the breach. Finally, however, worn down by the stubbornness of the defense and the unexpected thickness of the walls, the assault petered out. Mustapha called off the attack.

For the next five days, every piece of ordnance the Turks possessed rained down a barrage on the walls of Senglea and Birgu. The assault then began again on August 7, this time focused on Post of Castile in the walls of Birgu, the strongpoint that had frustrated Mustapha's first attempt in May.

A large breach was opened in the walls of Birgu, and the Turkish soldiers felt they had a certain victory pinned down. They poured through the hole in the defenses, all set either to die and attain paradise in the arms of beautiful *houris* or live in an orgy of slaughter, looting, and rapine.

Unfortunately, the breach in the walls of Birgu turned out to be a trap. A second wall had been constructed within the outer wall.

The janissaries found themselves caught in multiple crossfires from almost every conceivable angle from both walls. They broke and ran.

The secondary assault on Senglea under the command of the less competent Piali Pasha was, astoundingly, more successful. La Valette, occupied completely with the massive attack on the Post of Castile, could send nothing across the bridge of boats between Birgu and the beleaguered southern peninsula to reinforce the garrison, seriously in danger of being overwhelmed.

The janissaries were thereby able to force an entry through a breach and won the outer defenses. They even managed to gain a position on the walls of the inner citadel itself.

The fall of Senglea was now only moments away. With Senglea taken, the Turks could pour across the pontoon bridge and into the heart of the Knights' defenses in minutes.

Unbelievably, with victory in their hands, the Ottoman army at that moment heard the trumpet call to retreat. The Turks not only pulled back from the assault, they went into full retreat back to their base camp at Marsa, the southern portion of the Grand Harbor.

The reason for this completely unexpected turn of events was that Mustapha had just received word that the Knights' long-awaited relief force had arrived. They were reportedly attacking Marsa preliminary to taking the Turks in the rear while the Turks were engaged with all their forces on the frontal attack. Panic-stricken messengers told of troops of Christian cavalry running through the camp killing all the inhabitants and burning everything in sight.

There was no relief force. On hearing the tumult of what had to be a major attempt by the Turks, a small cavalry detachment from forgotten Mdina decided to create a diversion and possibly draw off a few attackers by sweeping down on the Ottoman base.

With every available man the Turks had thrown into the assaults at Birgu and Senglea, the camp held little but supplies, a few guards, and the sick and wounded with their attendants. Cavalry from Mdina under the command of

Captain Vincenzo Anastagi attacked and killed most of the inhabitants, set fire to a number of tents and storage depots, and hamstrung or made off with the horses. They then hurried back to Mdina, having carried out, as they thought, a gallant little sortie to take some of the pressure off of the main defense force.

They had done more than that. By a providential set of circumstances, they had duplicated the Sieur de Guiral's almost miraculous salvation of Senglea, forcing Mustapha to withdraw from what was by then an all but complete victory. Once again the Ottoman general tore at his beard in mortification and frustration.

La Valette's advisors came up with the suggestion, reasonable enough given the condition of the peninsula and the fact that it had twice been nearly overrun, that Senglea be abandoned. They suggested that all the Knights and other fighting men withdraw to Birgu and the bridge of boats be destroyed.

La Valette, however, refused to leave the Maltese to the mercies of the Turk. He declared that the civilians, every man, woman, and child, had been as active in the defense of the island as any Knight or man-at-arms.

There was possibly more to this decision than simple honor, although that was, of course, of paramount importance. La Valette may have been aware that the great weaknesses of the Turkish attack to date had been caused by their split command structure.

The Turks had only achieved success when under the single leadership of the now dead Torghoud Rais. By forcing the Ottomans to continue to divide their efforts, the Grand Master very likely saved Malta.

At about this time, la Valette received yet one more promise of a relief force from Don Garcia de Toledo, but put no stock in it. On the contrary, when the council next met, he informed them that they could expect no relief.

From that point on, there would be no retreat. The bridge of boats between Senglea and Birgu was dismantled and the drawbridge that linked Castle Saint Angelo and Birgu proper was blown up.

Instead of one objective that had to be overcome, the Turks now had three, each of which would have to be overcome individually. And each objective was by itself much stronger than Castle Saint Elmo had ever been.

Time was running out for the invaders, and they knew it. The storms of autumn would soon be on them, making resupply and reinforcement as well as retreat all but impossible.

Mustapha Pasha redoubled his efforts. The new isolation of Senglea made it virtually useless for his purposes, so Birgu became the focus of Turkish attacks.

Mines were dug through the solid limestone of the island to bring down the critical strongpoint of the Post of Castile. Most of these were countermined in classic fashion by the defenders.

Malvoisin—"Bad Neighbor," as the mobile siege towers were called—were put to use, but to very little effect. The Knights made sorties out of hidden sally ports cut in their own walls and burned or chopped down the machines before they could do any harm.

On August 18, Turkish efforts reached a new pitch. A mine exploded under the Post of Castile and a huge breach opened in the main bastion.

Poised for the attack, massed janissaries poured into the undefended gap before the dust settled. For an instant, the Knights and their men-at-arms hesitated. It seemed as if there might be a panic and sudden retreat.

At that moment, la Valette, seventy years old and armed only with the great double-handed sword of the Order, with no armor other than a light skirmish helmet, leaped into the fight. Around him rallied Knights, men-at-arms, militia, and citizens, charging into the breach at a dead run and fighting hand-to-hand with the Turks.

A grenade explosion wounded the Grand Master in the leg, but he refused to leave the fight, although urged by aides to save his own life. Realizing that it was his presence alone that put heart into the defense, he pointed to the Turkish standards that had been placed in the breach. With his almost preternatural instinct for the dramatic, he declared that he would never withdraw as long as the Ottoman banners stayed. The Turks again retreated.

Contrary to usual Turkish custom, the attack was renewed that night, with supporting fire from Ottoman galleys in the Grand Harbor, daring for the first time to come within range of the guns of Castle Saint Angelo. This attack, too, failed, but it seemed now as if the siege would go in favor of the invaders.

By the third week in August, every bed in the Great Hospital was filled with the sick and wounded. Ammunition was running short.

Anyone who could walk was not considered wounded. Some could barely do that, but still dragged themselves to their posts, much like the two defenders of Castle Saint

Elmo who had themselves conveyed to the crumbling walls in carrying chairs and propped up to fight to the last.

The Turks had unwisely made camp too near the stagnant waters of a swamp, and disease was making its way through the camp at Marsa. Their own supplies were running low, dysentery was rampant, and, worst of all, morale was flagging. Not even the promise of paradise could incite the janissaries and *sipahis* to greater efforts.

Further, the two commanders were once again arguing. Piali Pasha was becoming anxious over the coming change in weather, while Mustapha Pasha wanted to continue the siege into winter, when victory would be, as he thought, certain. Neither commander seemed aware that the Turks were already beaten by the extremely effective joint efforts of the Knights and the Maltese, as well as by the tenacious spirit of the defenders.

Desperation and ingenuity now took the place of military science, always in short supply with the two surviving Ottoman commanders. Had Torghoud Rais survived, it is entirely possible that Castle Saint Angelo would have fallen weeks before, but neither Mustapha nor Piali seemed able to bring the siege to the desired conclusion. Mines, petards, rolling firebombs (some of which destroyed the Turks rather than their targets), malvoisin loaded with harquebusiers . . . anything that seemed as if it might work was put in play.

On September 6, Don Garcia de Toledo finally arrived with his by-now unexpected relief force. The storms of autumn had already begun, and the fleet had encountered great difficulty making even the short voyage from Sicily to Malta.

At a paltry eight thousand or so troops, the relief was far below what would have been needed for an effective campaign against the still-powerful Turkish army, but it was enough to break the spirit of the Ottoman offensive. After landing at Mellieha Bay in the northeast of Malta, word quickly spread of the reinforcements as they marched to Mdina. Maltese peasants judiciously exaggerated their numbers, which were then reported as established fact by panic-stricken Turkish scouts.

For once in complete accord, Mustapha and Piali agreed to lift the siege immediately and head for home as fast as possible. The morning of September 7 found the Turks breaking camp and moving as fast as possible to their ships, while the siege was officially lifted on September 8, the Feast of the Nativity of the Blessed Virgin.

When the bells of Saint Lawrence in Birgu and those of the Church of Our Lady in Senglea pealed out the victory, it was the first time in weeks that they had rung for anything except to signal another attack. A solemn *Te Deum*, a special thanksgiving service, was offered, and people came out from behind the defenses and toured the shattered landscape around Birgu and Senglea, filled with the wreckage and detritus of battle, along with numbers of the dead whom the enemy had not taken the time to bury before pulling out.

It was not long before Mustapha Pasha learned of the real numbers of the relief force. He immediately attempted to rally his men and return to the attack. Unfortunately, many of them had already re-embarked in the fleet that was now at anchor in Saint Paul's Bay on the east coast of the island. It was too late to turn the men around and go back to the seemingly endless fighting. They refused to obey.

The Turkish soldiers had had enough. The Knights Hospitallers of the Order of Saint John of Jerusalem, of Rhodes, and of Malta, the "Sons of Shaitan," and the people of Malta had defeated the unconquerable armies of the Prophet.

Hoping that it would give Süleymân the Magnificent time to calm down and accept the situation, Piali and Mustapha were canny enough to send word of the defeat ahead in a swift galley. For once, they had judged the situation correctly.

Although Süleymân had trained himself to accept all news, good or bad, with composure, receiving word of the defeat at Malta caused him to be shaken out of his carefully cultivated air of detachment and indifference. Baffled and enraged, the great Ottoman lawgiver is reputed to have exclaimed, "I see now that it is only in mine own hand that my sword is invincible."

Never one to rest either on his laurels or lack thereof, as well as completely uninhibited by any feeling of inferiority, Süleymân immediately gave orders to prepare for another invasion of "the accursed island" of Malta. This would take place the following year, and he would lead the invasion in person. He swore by the bones of his fathers that he would not spare anyone.

The sultan's mighty vow to the contrary, however, the Turks never again seriously threatened the island.

HISTORICAL NOTE: THROUGH THE GATES OF BLISS

Outside the walls of Istanbul, near a lower-class district called Davut Pasa, was a meadow. This was normally used for pasturing the flocks belonging to the ubiquitous nomads. From the fifteenth until the nineteenth century, when the janissaries were disbanded, however, the field was turned into a tent city every year immediately following Ramadan. This was the sultan's war camp.

Once the encampment had been completed, down to the last detail a recreation of a typical Ottoman city, even to the sultan's seraglio or harem, the janissaries raised a gilded staff bearing the war standard in front of the sultan's tent. This was the signal for the fighting men of the empire to assemble.

Each *beylerbey,* or "beglar bey," as the provincial governors were called, mustered a contingent of *sipahis*, the Turkish heavy cavalry, each of whom held their *timars,* or fiefs, in return for military service. Each *sipahi* furnished his own horse and equipment, rather like the Roman republican equestrian class. *Sipahis* were analogous to the famed Polish *hussaria*, from whom western Europe derived its hussars, similar in name though not in function.

The *sipahis* were usually armed with both a saber for close-in fighting and a long straight sword for charges. These weapons were typically inherited from fathers and grandfathers. As late as the eighteenth century, *sipahis* wore steel breastplates over coats of mail and plumed steel helmets.

As the weeks passed, long columns of horsemen converged on the Golden Horn. Most of these were *sipahis*, but would also include *akinjis*, the irregular, lightly armed raiders.

Infantry units included companies of *segmens* or sharp-shooters who were armed with harquebuses and short swords. There were also the *tüfekçis* or harquebusiers, typically dressed in short red coats and tall red conical hats. Bands of Tartar light cavalry, armed with their short but powerful compound bows and each one accompanied with his string of spare ponies, could usually be counted on to appear in large numbers.

As detachments came in, they would be listed and checked against the muster roles. Each *sipahi* would pass inspection. Every firearm was carefully checked. All rations were sealed and certified by imperial officials.

At the center of the camp was the sultan's pavilion, surrounded by the quarters of the janissaries and the sultan's household troops. Specific times were set aside each day for drilling. This consisted of massed charges and the firing of guns in the face of the opposing side.

Beyond the imperial enclosure, each *orta*, or regiment, arranged its tents in a grid around the regimental cooking pot. Dispossession of the common cauldron was a mark of shame akin to the ancient Spartan who lost his shield.

Even further away were the *kapikulu süvarileri*, the sultan's household cavalry. Unlike the *sipahis*, these were equipped at the sultan's expense. They had the finest horses and were well armed with lance, sword, or bow, defending themselves with heavy chain mail coats and capped with turbans wrapped around spiked metal helmets.

The Turkish muster was not just a military event, however. It was a religious ritual that went to the heart of what it meant to be an Ottoman Muslim.

When the sultan's standard, the *Tug*, decorated with bells and horsetails, was paraded through the streets, people threw themselves face down on the ground. As the sacred banner of the Prophet was taken from its special chamber in the palace and unwrapped from its forty silk coverings, the crowds bowed before it and invoked the name of Allah.

The symbols of Islam made the camp of war a holy place. The war it announced became *jihad*, a sacred duty for every man capable of bearing arms.

7

SZIGETVÁR

1566

AUTUMN 1565 was a gloomy season in Istanbul. The city on the Bosphorus had once been the capital of the Eastern Roman Empire. For over a century now, however, it had been the center of the Ottoman Empire. The market rabble had become accustomed to a splendid parade of slaves and loot from the summer campaigning season. There was the added inducement of the generosity of the Protector of the Poor and the Leader of the Faithful, Sultan Süleymân the Magnificent, perhaps the greatest ruler the Turks were ever to know.

This year was different. There was no victory to celebrate.

Instead, terrible news had arrived of a great debacle on the island of Malta. This was a seemingly insignificant outpost in the western Mediterranean, occupied by a handful of warrior monks and a crowd of insignificant peasants.

Despite that, three-quarters of an invasion force made up of the cream of the Turkish army, thirty-one thousand men out of an estimated forty-five thousand, had died attempting to establish a beachhead in western Europe. The survivors were racked with illness and wounds.

Never had the Turkish armies under Süleymân or any other sultan suffered such a calamity. To make matters

The River Fortress of Szigetvár

Tisza River

N

Maros River

Inner
Fortress

Outer
Fortress

Keep

worse, the defeat had been inflicted by a force they outnumbered nearly six to one.

Although he had trained himself to receive all news, good
or bad, with complete indifference, Süleymân the Magnificent was shocked. Conveniently forgetting his defeat at the
Siege of Vienna in 1529, he exclaimed that now he understood his sword was invincible only in his own hand.

Plans were immediately set afoot to avenge the humiliation inflicted by the Sovereign Military and Hospitaller Order of Saint John of Jerusalem, of Rhodes, and of Malta (the "Knights of Malta") and their Maltese allies. Süleymân the Conqueror was not only out for revenge, he was under a religious mandate to extend Islam—at least as the Turks understood the matter.

Having sworn to exact a terrible revenge on Malta, Süleymân immediately set to work. His task would not be easy.

The chief difficulty was that, since the Ottoman state required constant infusions of loot from military victories to remain economically viable, there was a considerable financing problem as a direct result of the disaster. There was also the difficulty that after a lifetime of so much going right for Süleymân the Magnificent, things had started going wrong. . . .

THE HUNGARIAN ALAMO

For the first time in Süleymân the Magnificent's reign, war had failed to pay for itself. The Maltese expedition had been one of the best equipped and, consequently, one of the most expensive of the sultan's career.

Without the regular infusion of precious metals or the creation of productive wealth that accompanied the availability of liquid capital, the economic and political stability of the Ottoman Empire was seriously shaken. In a self-defeating attempt to bolster the economy and finance the next venture, the sultan ordered that the gold coinage from the mints in Egypt be debased by putting less gold and more copper in each coin.

The projected cost of a second attack on Malta was great, but the prize was immense. The sultan's goal was nothing less than the opening of a new gateway into western Europe. Consequently, Süleymân ordered a new expedition for the following year. This expedition, as Süleymân declared, was one that he would lead himself. He swore by the bones of his fathers (a favorite oath) that he would not spare a single human life.

There was no attack.

The reason was simple. The main powder magazine in Istanbul, the Grand Arsenal that housed the immense stores of gunpowder that had been accumulated for the expedition, exploded. What was not lost in the blast itself was destroyed in the fire that followed.

While the explosion could very well have been caused accidentally (common enough in those days), many historians and contemporaries preferred to credit the disaster to Jean Parisot de la Valette, reigning Grand Master of the Order of Malta. Rumor spread that he had sent spies to destroy the Turks' ability to make war, at least against Malta in the near future, and they had been spectacularly successful.

The truth of the matter will never be known. It is, however, highly unlikely that spies, however clever and resourceful, would have been able to infiltrate one of the most secure military installations in the entire Ottoman Empire, especially on the eve of an important campaign.

Whatever the real cause of the explosion, the gunpowder was irreplaceable. The money simply was not there to resupply another effort to conquer an island that had already held off the best troops the empire could field, and at such hideous cost.

Süleymân the Magnificent therefore postponed his revenge on Malta, at least for the foreseeable future. Instead, with the diplomatic encouragement of his tacit allies, the French, the sultan decided to attack Hungary.

Hungary was at that time severely weakened and degenerated from its past glory but still a strategically important gateway into central Europe. It was also the gateway to the Holy Roman Empire and the Polish-Lithuanian Commonwealth, both of which constantly vied with France for control of Europe. The French were not averse to anything that stood a chance of diminishing the power of their two great rivals.

Hungary was a supremely logical choice for Süleymân the Magnificent. Ever since the battle of Mohács in 1526, the sultan had viewed what was left of the country as his private preserve. For decades, he had looted it almost at will for men, material, and virtually every known form of portable wealth, including vast numbers of slaves. Needing funds, there was no better place to stage a profitable expedition.

Only a portion of the country, however, was under the suzerainty of the Turks. The rest was partitioned among the other great powers. Accordingly, the Turks considered the region fair game for pillaging and slave raiding.

Hungary was, at that time, at the very limits of Turkish logistical and administrative reach. It would, of course, have been possible to devolve authority and extend that reach almost infinitely, as both the Persians and the Spanish had done with empires that stretched over immense geographic areas.

The Ottoman Empire, however, through its political structure and tendency to set father against son while decisions and changes were made in the succession, required an absolute centralization of authority. Anything beyond the personal reach of the sultan was, effectively, beyond anything more than the temporary reach of the empire. Even the sultan's principal lieutenants could not really be trusted given the nature of the political arrangements. In many respects, it was a far worse situation than that which prevailed in the old Roman Empire, where authority was nominally vested in the Senate and not whoever was Caesar.

The capital city of Hungary, Buda, had been taken and occupied a number of times by the Turks, most recently in 1541. This was the result of one of Süleymân the Magnificent's more spectacular campaigns.

The city was located in the central and most fertile part of the country, the Great Plain. Pesth, the suburb across the river, was yet to be incorporated into the ancient capital. The supreme ruler of the Hungarian territory after its inclusion as part of the Ottoman Empire was a beglar bey. Having the official title of pasha, this provincial governor was directly responsible to the sultan.

The Turkish system of taxation put an extraordinarily heavy burden on the Hungarian serfs. They were not allowed to change residence without permission or travel anywhere except the local neighborhood without a passport or specific orders. They were not allowed to build stone houses or repair damaged dwellings without explicit permission. In order to ensure a steady supply of slave soldiers, the famed janissaries, the population was permitted to remain Christian—fellow Muslims could not be enslaved for service in the sultan's army.

Thus, whenever the sultan felt a need to replenish his purse, he generally raided Hungary. After Mohács and the tripartite division among the Holy Roman Empire, the Polish-Lithuanian Commonwealth, and the Turks, Hungary was not able to mount an effective resistance against the Ottomans.

The Holy Roman Empire, weakened by internal dissension as a result of the Reformation and by conflicts with France, was not able to retake the country. The emperor had to be satisfied with maintaining Hungary as a frontier region.

The Polish-Lithuanian Commonwealth lacked a coherent and stable internal political structure. It was thus unable to extend its influence much further than it already had.

Hungary was therefore left pretty much to its own devices. This was ironic, for western and northern Europe still relied on the country to provide a firm defense against the Eastern menace.

After Mohács, the western and northern areas of Hungary had come under the rule of Ferdinand of Hapsburg. This was the area termed "the Kingdom of Hungary."

Ferdinand was the brother of Charles V. He had been assigned responsibility for the eastern portion of Charles's vast dominions. Ferdinand's goal was the unification of Austria, Bohemia, and Hungary under one strong, central government. While he never succeeded completely, his efforts resulted in a strengthening of the front line defenses against the Turk that ran through the middle of Hungary.

By 1566, after Ferdinand and Charles had both passed from the scene, a network of fortresses similar to the ancient *Limes*, Rome's barbarian frontier, had been created. Troops were stationed behind the lines ready to move in whatever direction expedience or necessity demanded, as had been the case with the late Roman *limitanei*. The line of fortresses along the border was the scene of continual skirmishes between the Holy Roman imperial forces and the Ottomans. There was a virtually permanent stalemate, for the European powers lacked the resources to do more than hold their own, and the Turks were not quite ready to conquer that particular area—and probably could not have sustained the logistical effort had they done so.

In addition, the current Holy Roman emperor, Maximilian II, had his hands full trying to hold together an empire torn by both religious and civil strife in the wake of the controversies initiated by Martin Luther half a century before. To this was added the traditional jockeying for power between the Holy Roman Empire, the kingdom of the French, and the Polish-Lithuanian Commonwealth.

This, then, was the setting for Süleymân the Magnificent's looting expedition into *Mitteleuropa* to raise money for another assault on Malta. The idea was to march to Buda, the capital, and then, using the Hungarian city as a base, force a showdown with the Roman armies in a climactic battle.

This would not only justify levying tribute in the form of men for the army and precious metals for the treasury over a wider area but also open up a clear road to Vienna, a life-long goal of the sultan. If the Ottoman Empire was

ever to expand deep into Europe, the eventual capture of
Vienna was an absolute necessity—after taking revenge on
Malta, of course. Vienna remained *the* target of the Turks for centuries.
Had the Turks succeeded in taking either Vienna or Malta,
the other would have fallen almost immediately. Western Europe would have been crushed in a gigantic pincer
movement.

The justification for the campaign was to support the
claims of John Sigismund Zápolya, the pretender to the
imperial crown, usually referred to as "Sigismund" to distinguish him from the earlier John Zápolya, also a Turkish collaborator. Having failed to receive support from
the Catholic powers in the empire in his bid for the purple, Sigismund had recently decided to turn Protestant. A
protégé of Süleymân, he had offered the sultan homage.

The Ottoman forces thus attempted to portray themselves as liberators and champions of the rightful heir to the
Holy Roman Empire. It seemed to make little difference
that the imperial diadem was not hereditary but elective,
and Sigismund had lost the election.

Süleymân the Magnificent was also apparently unaware
that his Turks were finally recognized as a far more serious
threat than the quarrels between Catholic and Protestant.
Even Elizabeth I of England, certainly no friend of the pope
or any of the Catholic powers, had already demonstrated
that she (or, at any rate, her advisors) knew the identity of
the real enemy. After the siege of Malta had been lifted,
she had ordered her archbishop of Canterbury to declare
a "Form of Thanksgiving" in all English churches "thrice
weekly for six weeks" in celebration of the victory.

Nevertheless, Süleymân the Magnificent hoped to capitalize on the religious and civil conflicts in Europe to open the way for his conquest of the entire continent. He had evidently forgotten, or never knew, that even a small number of Jews, disillusioned by the harrowing reception often granted their people by the Turks after their expulsion from Spain, and despite their hatred of the Christians, had fought on the side of the Knights at Malta against the Ottoman army.

Apparently anything—even restrictions on daily life, heavy monetary fines, and possible persecution and exile—was to be preferred to the all-too-real horrors of life for a non-Turk (and many Turks and other Muslims as well) under Ottoman rule. Adding that miscalculation to the almost unbelievable morale boost of having a mere handful of Knights and men-at-arms defeat the hitherto invincible Turk at Malta, and you had a bad situation that could only be ignored by a combination of optimism and contempt for a foe who had managed only once in history to go against him.

Even so, Süleymân hedged his bets. In spite of his miscalculations, he was far from stupid. He wanted to take no chances on his ability to sweep all opposition from his path.

He collected an army estimated at three hundred thousand and set to work. This was a force far larger than anything the combined peoples of Europe could possibly field, even though many of the sultan's men were slave conscripts intended to serve as engineers and cannon fodder.

Although Süleymân would accompany the army into Hungary, direct command was vested in his recently promoted grand vizier, Mehmet Sokolli. Sokolli was an experienced hand in the Balkans. Not only had he campaigned there extensively, he had grown up in Sokolic in Bosnia, whence he derived his Islamic name, before he turned renegade and entered the sultan's service.

Sokolli's father was an Orthodox priest. He was not illegitimate; Orthodox priests are permitted to marry before they take orders, although bishops are drawn exclusively from the ranks of celibate monks.

Being much too old and feeble to ride as befitted a commander of the faithful, except on rare occasions, Süleymân rode in a carriage or was carried in a curtained litter. Sources claim both, but the litter seems more probable.

The progress of the army carefully matched the capabilities of the sultan. It took forty-three days to reach Nándorfehérvár (Belgrade).

In addition to the slow pace necessitated by Süleymân's condition, the march had been prolonged due to constant attacks by "bandits." These were native partisans who took the opportunity to raid the supply train and cut off stragglers.

Although they had recently welcomed the Ottomans as liberators, the common people had quickly become disillusioned. They were oppressed by the growing poverty and tax burden, especially the requirement to surrender their children to the sultan's harem and army. Gibbets decorated with the bodies of those who had been captured after a remorseless hunt lined the army's route for miles.

The Turks picked up Sigismund along the way, just in case a pretext was needed to commence hostilities. Süleymân had acknowledged Sigismund's claim to the ephemeral kingdom of Hungary while the pretender was still a child.

The young man now knelt three times in a show of fealty to his master, kissed the sultan's hand, and was proclaimed a Beloved Son. Knowing that he would have a willing puppet in Sigismund, Süleymân made a public announcement that he would not cease the struggle until the crown of Hungary rested on Sigismund's brow, and the road to Vienna lay open.

To all appearances, the Turks would march straight into the heart of Hungary, gathering wealth and sweeping all before them to open up a gateway into the Holy Roman Empire. They would finally take Vienna.

Europe was doomed.

Neither the Turks nor the Christians, however, counted on the bravado, self-sacrifice, and sheer raw courage of one Count Miklós Zrinyi.

Count Zrinyi was a Croatian-Hungarian nobleman whose family possessed huge estates that stretched from the Transdanube region to the Adriatic. Miklós himself, referred to as "the general" to distinguish him from his grandson the poet, had been a bitter enemy of the Turks since the siege of Vienna in 1529 and the attempted siege of 1532.

The count, now commander of the fortress of Szigetvár, staged a daring raid on a Turkish contingent commanded by a *sanjak bey*, a regional governor and favorite of the sultan. The *sanjak bey* and his son were killed, while Zrinyi made off with all the man's possessions and seventeen thousand ducats (gold thalers or dollars, each worth two of the silver denomination).

Süleymân the Magnificent was outraged. Turkish rule, based firmly on a foundation of terror, could brook no such effrontery.

Atypically—and unwisely—letting his emotions get the better of his judgment and military genius, the sultan ordered a complete change of plans. Virtually the whole of the Turkish army was to take itself to Szigetvár immediately. Once there, orders were to wipe the fortress off the face of the earth—a minor matter. There would be plenty of time to attack Buda and enthrone Süleymân's puppet with the crown as king of Hungary.

Almost superhuman effort was required to fulfill Süleymân's new orders. An enormous pontoon bridge that took seventeen days to construct was thrown across the Drava River. A fleet of war galleys then had to be rowed up the Danube. Finally, by July 19, the Turks had made the crossing, the sultan hard on their heels. Süleymân reached Szigetvár on August 5, the last leg of the journey being accomplished in one day instead of two due to the over-enthusiasm of a quartermaster.

Angered, the sultan ordered the quartermaster's immediate decapitation. Sokolli saved the man's life with the exercise of a little judicious flattery. He pointed out that when the Christians saw that Süleymân, presumably feeble with age, had taken one day where ordinary men would take two, they would be utterly terrified of his astonishing strength and vigor. To assuage his feelings, however, Süleymân ordered the execution of his governor of Buda for incompetence.

Sokolli had already invested Szigetvár before Süleymân's arrival, surrounding the town and fortress with ninety thousand men. The walls of the town were under constant bombardment from three hundred cannon that Sokolli had placed on a nearby hill.

When Count Zrinyi learned that Süleymân the Magnificent had arrived in camp, he raised a giant crucifix on the highest point of the fortress where the entire Turkish army could see it. With his own guns, he punctiliously fired off the correct formal salute for an Ottoman sultan. He also raised a black flag, letting the besiegers know that he and all his men expected to die to the last man before letting the Turks set one foot inside the fortress.

Having had a good look at the town and castle, Süleymân may have had second thoughts about the wisdom of having diverted his attack, particularly for what could only be construed as a non-military mission of revenge.

The town would obviously be a tough nut to crack. It was situated on a series of islands in the middle of a tributary of the Drava, which served as a moat protecting two sides of the town. Taking the town would involve hard fighting simply to cross any one of the bridges that led to the three islands on which the town was built.

If the town would be difficult, the fortress itself would be next to impossible. Built of brick, it was surrounded by five earthen ramparts. Earthen walls, as the Austrians had discovered during the 1529 siege of Vienna, were much more effective at stopping cannon balls than any other kind of defense. To storm the castle, the Turks would have to engage in close-order fighting in the town, charge uphill no less than five times, cross four small valleys with strategically placed crossfires, breach the outer stone walls of the castle, and, finally, assault the inner citadel.

All in all, it was a daunting prospect. The cost was certain to be high. It is no wonder that Sokolli first attempted standard, if outdated, siege tactics in an effort to reduce the fortress. Unfortunately for him, this was precisely what Count Zrinyi had expected him to do, and the effort played right into the defenders' hands.

Making certain that the Turks knew the difficulties inherent in what they were about to essay, Count Zrinyi hung bolts of red cloth on the outer ramparts as a sign of defiance, while huge sheets of tin decorated the tower of the citadel, flashing and glittering in the sun. The whole gave the fortress the aspect of having been prepared for a festival.

There was more than madness in the count's method. Outnumbered by more than a hundred to one, he needed every possible morale boost to encourage the garrison.

While the Turks might be incensed enough to carry the town by storm, it would be costly. The butcher's bill for the castle and the inner citadel would be greater still. There was thus a very real possibility that the ill-considered siege could bog down the Turkish campaign in a strategically useless endeavor. This would either buy enough time for defenses elsewhere to be strengthened or cause the Turks to retreat before the onset of winter made travel—and war—impossible.

Even more infuriating to Süleymân was the fact that the whole situation had begun to take on definite aspects of the prior year's disaster at Malta.

The Turks were encamped in a swampy area, and fever was already beginning to take its toll. They were faced with a strongly held position, and, worse, Count Zrinyi was clearly aware that this was his chance for immortality and eternal glory.

With the example of the defenders of Malta ever before his eyes, the count knew that those of all Christendom would soon be upon him and his 2,500 comrades in arms. At one stroke, he could avenge and restore the honor of his God, his country, his family, and himself. As far as Miklós Zrinyi was concerned, it was the Turks who should be worried, not he.

It would have gratified Zrinyi immensely to know that his hopes were completely fulfilled by the enemy. Both he and the Turks knew that he could not be conquered except by death, which, as Winston Churchill later observed about the Saxons at the battle of Hastings, does not count in honor (i.e., death is no dishonor; only running away is), and that the return to the attacker would be very small indeed.

By sacrificing men lavishly, the Turks took the town in fifteen days. Fighting every inch of the way, Count Zrinyi ordered the houses surrounding the fortress destroyed when they could no longer be held.

Into the smoking ruins of the town, the Turks hauled siege guns drawn by huge teams of water buffalo. There they positioned the cannon at point blank range and continued to bombard the castle walls.

In an effort to cut the siege short and free the troops for the march on Buda, Sokolli initiated some clever psychological warfare. He was fully aware that the castle garrison consisted of a number of different races, nationalities, and religions. There were Germans, Croats, Hungarians, and, possibly, Cossacks and renegade Tartars.

An even more volatile mix was represented by the fact that the Christians were divided between Catholics, Protestants, and Orthodox. As noted earlier, they were joined by Jews and Muslims who feared the tyranny of the Turk far more than the bigotry of the Christians.

Sokolli ordered propaganda letters in various languages shot over the walls by arrow, hoping to win over the Protestants by playing on the religious differences—he viewed Catholics as the more serious threat. He then made a secret offer to Count Zrinyi: at the price of the surrender of Sziget-vár, he could be governor of all Croatia.

Count Zrinyi pretended to consider the offer as long as he could. Finally even Sokolli, optimistic about the count's self-interest, could see that he was stalling.

Sokolli ordered an assault on August 26. To the utter amazement of the Turks, the first massed attack was beaten back.

Sokolli waited a few days before ordering another attack. The chosen day, August 29, was the anniversary of Süley-mân's great victory at Mohács, where, as the Hungarians relate, their national hopes and greatness were destroyed for centuries.

Again, the attack was a stunning reversal of Turkish expectations. Süleymân, sick with dysentery, wrote a note to the grand vizier: "This chimney still burns, and the drum of conquest has yet to be heard."

Sokolli then switched tactics. He set sappers to work under the walls of the fortress.

Finally, on September 5, a huge mine blew up the grand bastion of the castle. This started an enormous fire and left the inner citadel wide open to attack. Sokolli planned a fresh assault early the next morning, but during the night, Süleymân the Magnificent died. The grand vizier was faced with an untenable situation. If news of the sultan's death leaked out, the attack was finished, his master's last wish unfulfilled.

Sokolli postponed the final assault and put out word that Süleymân was confined to his tent with an attack of gout. He is said even to have had the sultan's physician strangled to keep the secret.

The Turkish batteries continued to bombard the castle for four more days. The fortress was leveled except for one tower, and the garrison reduced to little more than six hundred survivors.

Having delayed the enemy long enough to derail the entire campaign and knowing the end was near, Count Zrinyi determined to die in style. He dressed in his finest clothes as if getting ready for a holiday and loaded himself with gold and jewels.

And he was certainly stylish. He put on a silk surtout (a long, close-fitting overcoat) and draped a gold chain around his neck. His hat was the best he had, embroidered with gold thread and decorated with a feather plume and a diamond brooch.

Despite his finery, Count Zrinyi put himself on an equal footing with the poorest man in the garrison and refused to wear armor. He contented himself with offensive rather than defensive arms, selecting the finest sword from among his collection.

Inspiring his men with the spirit of Christian martyrdom—which apparently did not faze the surviving Jews and Muslims one bit—the count made his final preparations for the battle. He drew his sword, inlaid with precious metals, and announced that he had won his first honors with it and was ready to appear with it before the throne of God for judgment.

Zrinyi ordered a large mortar filled to the brim with a deadly and chilling mix of scrap iron and laid a fuse to the main powder magazine at the base of the remaining tower. He placed the mortar directly behind the gate of the drawbridge leading to the tower, where any potential attacker would not be able to see it.

Nor had Sokolli been idle. Almost in a parody of Zrinyi's preparations, he dressed Süleymân in his best robes and fastened the corpse to the throne of the sultan. This was despite the fact that the body was quite likely some the worse for wear after four days of lingering without burial and an embalming under field conditions.

It did not matter, for no one would be close enough to observe the sultan's true condition . . . or so the grand vizier hoped. Sokolli had the front of the tent drawn back so that both attackers and defenders could observe Süleymân the Magnificent in his glory as he watched the final victory of his armies.

The grand vizier then ordered the assault. As the janissaries swarmed over the remaining defenses, Count Zrinyi opened the gate and fired the mortar, possibly (and characteristically) with his own hand.

Under the murderous rain of shrapnel, the attackers died by the hundreds, so closely packed were they as they poured through the breach. Drawing his weapon, the count and the surviving members of the garrison who had agreed to accompany him on his last charge counterattacked.

They fought to the last man. Count Zrinyi was struck
with two harquebus balls in the breast, and an arrow pierced
his skull. His final act was to fire the fuse to the powder magazine.
The explosion reportedly killed three thousand Turks—
more than the entire original garrison of the castle.
Another account states that Count Zrinyi did not manage
to light the fuse, but, even with the hideous wounds he suffered, was taken alive. He was tied down to a gun carriage
and his head cut off.

The severed head, allegedly still with its jeweled hat and
gold chain (although on what the chain supposedly hung is
a little unclear), was presented to Sokolli as a trophy. The
grand vizier, in retribution for the prolonged siege, then
gave the order to kill every Christian survivor of Szigetvár. This would presumably make up for the lack of looting
during the campaign and assuage the feelings of the troops
with a massacre.

Sokolli could now order a withdrawal, having salvaged
the honor of Süleymân the Magnificent and ensured the
peaceful accession of Prince Selim, the chosen heir. He
sent a messenger to Selim to go to Istanbul and assume
the throne immediately. The prince did so, assisted by others who had placed their bets on him: Piali Pasha, Joseph
Micas, and Lala Mustapha, each of whom began jockeying
for position and to displace the others.

The Turkish army now began the long march back to
Istanbul, the grand vizier giving out orders as if passing
them on from the sultan. He even had the army undertake a
minor siege along the way as if in conformity with Süleymân's wishes.

Carried in its covered litter, the guard and honors due a living Ottoman ruler were accorded the sultan's body. An Austrian force, which had been held at readiness at Györ in anticipation of an advance on Vienna, retired without striking a blow. Patriotic Hungarians have been slow to forgive this move, or failure to move, particularly in light of the heroic sacrifice made by Count Zrinyi and his men and their achievement in turning a Turkish walkover into a Pyrrhic victory. To be fair, however, it is difficult to understand what the Austrian troops could have hoped to accomplish in an attack on a superior and victorious foe, except to abandon their post and leave the way to Vienna wide open in the event of their defeat.

Sokolli did not announce the death of Süleymân the Magnificent until the Turks were camped outside Nán-dorfehérvár (Belgrade) and the grand vizier had received word that Selim had safely reached Istanbul. Süleymân was widely mourned as the greatest ruler the Turks would ever know—and rightly so.

Süleymân's own greatness, however, set the stage for the decline of the empire he had brought to its zenith. The system relied on the man, not on the inherent soundness of its institutions. Men of much lesser caliber and ability than himself would follow.

Süleymân's son and chosen successor would be held in open contempt and publicly referred to as "Selim the Drunk" by his own subjects for his alcohol addiction. It would be during Selim's reign that the Turks would suffer what many consider their single greatest defeat: the battle of Lepanto.

The career of Süleymân the Magnificent, particularly in its end, displayed the fundamental weakness in the Turkish system. This weakness was the very fact that the system was not, technically speaking, a system. It relied on a single man to keep things running, which meant that it would inevitably decay. The Ottoman Empire began its long decline almost immediately upon the death of Süleymân.

HISTORICAL NOTE: ARMORED INFANTRY

It is popularly supposed that gunpowder spelled the end of the supremacy of the medieval knight and ushered in the twilight of the age of chivalry. Nothing could be further from the truth.

What brought the end of heavily armored cavalry were better infantry tactics and improved weapons, notably the eighteen- to twenty-foot pike. Swiss mercenaries, whose modern descendants make up the Vatican's Swiss Guard, developed the weapons and the tactics probably in the early fifteenth century.

By the end of the fifteenth century, the new style of warfare had proved so effective that German mercenaries began adopting it. In 1487, prior to his election as Holy Roman emperor, Maximilian I organized the first *Landsknechten* ("countryside infantry") regiments with the help of Georg von Frundsburg, *Vater des Landsknechts* ("Father of the Landsknecht"). Taking part in every major European battle in the 1500s, the *Landsknechten* ruled the battlefields of central and western Europe throughout the sixteenth century.

The idea was simple and relatively easy. Soldiers would group themselves in a defensive position with their long pikes pointing outward in all uncovered directions. Having one's back against the wall was a good thing if the defenses held, as it cut off one line of possible attack by the enemy. And there they would stay. Against a "hedgehog formation" of pikemen supported by other infantry, cavalry was virtually useless. Given the length of the new pole weapons, a horse and rider would be impaled before getting close enough to do any damage.

That did not mean an infantry formation was invincible, however. When not in formation and on the move, they could easily be overcome by cavalry.

Lack of mobility was the great weakness of the hedgehog formation. Practically invulnerable while standing their ground, they were ineffective if the enemy did not attack.

There were, however, ways to break up infantry formations. If artillery could be brought to bear, a few well-placed shots were almost guaranteed to do the trick.

The problem was that the artillery of the day was only slightly more mobile than a hedgehog formation. It had to be carefully sited before it was much use. Its effective use in the field by the Turks, as at the battle of Mohács, was relatively rare; it was primarily a siege weapon.

There was another way to break up formed infantry, although it strikes people familiar with modern methods of warfare as a little insane. A number of heavily armored infantry armed with short sword and dagger would volunteer (no officer would order a man to do this) to lie down on the ground and roll into the enemy formation under the pikes.

Assuming the line of pikes did not stop them, and support infantry did not kill them once they were inside the defensive screen, the volunteers would get to their feet and begin killing as many of the enemy as they could. If the pikemen dropped their pikes to defend themselves, the formation would break up and the cavalry could charge. If the formation included non-pikemen to counter such tactics, the effort usually failed.

It was not until the invention of improved firearms that could be reloaded relatively quickly and fired easily that armored infantry began to fade from the scene. The appearance of field artillery that could be moved rapidly during a battle ensured both their demise and the rise of new infantry tactics.

8

NICOSIA

1570

CYPRUS, the third largest island in the Mediterranean, is strategically located in the sea's far eastern corner. With Syria to the east, Turkey to the north, Egypt to the south, and Greece to the west, it is ideally situated to take maximum advantage of both the east-west and the north-south trade routes. It also has valuable products of its own, especially copper in former times (deposits of which, now largely exhausted, gave the island its name), sugar, cotton, and wine.

For over eight millennia, these unique advantages have subjected the island to a series of invasions, occupations, and conquests hard to match by any area of equally small size. By the latter half of the sixteenth century, Cyprus had been continuously occupied since Neolithic times.

Saint Paul and Saint Barnabas introduced Christianity circa AD 45–46 and converted Sergius Paulus, the Roman proconsul of Paphos. This led to a great many other conversions, and, by the third century, virtually the entire population was Christian.

Cypriot legend has it that the island enjoyed the favor of Constantine the Great and, especially, his mother, Saint Helena, who is said to have endowed many of the churches and monasteries. A delegation from Cyprus to the First Council of Nicea in 325 helped ensure the condemnation of the Arian heresy. Subsequent emperors continued to favor Cyprus and grant privileges to its Church, with the result that the island achieved *de facto* political neutrality. With the rise of Islam, however, Cyprus's neutral status caused it to become a pawn in the struggle between the Byzantine Empire and the Arabs.

Arab raiders managed to establish enclaves in some parts of Cyprus that they used to launch attacks on the empire as well as other parts of the island. As had been the case in a number of places in Europe, civil authority broke down and the Church was forced to take over the job of governance.

The Byzantine re-conquest of 963–64 reestablished the civil government and suppressed some ecclesiastical privileges. The imperial government, however, more than compensated the Church by sponsoring and endowing a large number of religious foundations.

As a result of the internecine strife following Manzikert, Isaac Comnenus, a great-nephew of Basileus Manuel I, escaped a reign of terror instituted by Andronicus Comnenus and set up an independent state on Cyprus. Isaac took the title basileus and struck his own coinage. The Byzantine Empire, too weak to defend even its internal integrity, lost Cyprus forever.

During the Third Crusade, Richard the Lionheart easily captured Cyprus by means of an invasion launched from Byzantium, imprisoned Isaac, and secured the crusaders' line of supply for the siege of Acre. Richard subsequently turned the island over to the Knights Templar, who sold

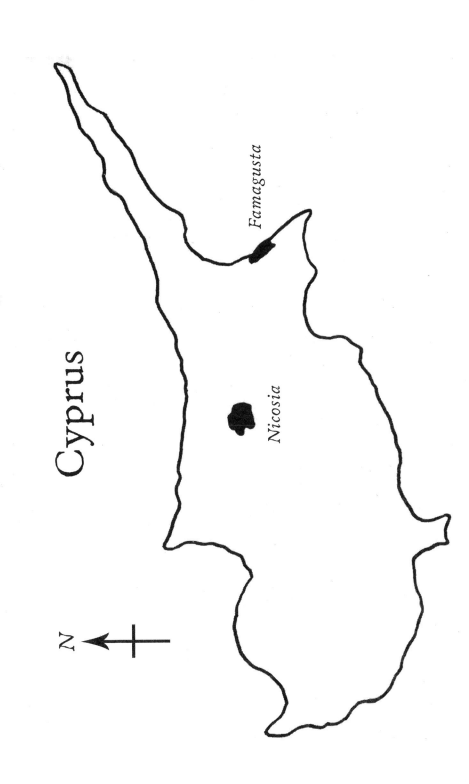

City of Nicosia

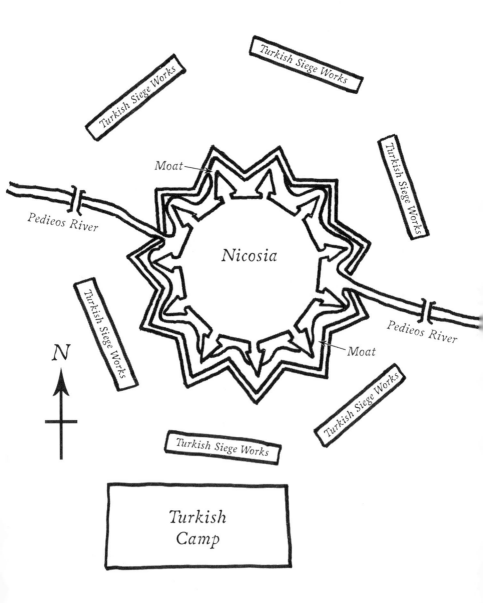

Turkish Siege Works

Turkish Siege Works

Turkish Siege Works

Moat

Pedieos River

Nicosia

Turkish Siege Works

Pedieos River

Moat

Turkish Siege Works

N

Turkish Siege Works

Turkish Camp

it in 1192 to Guy of Lusignan, the French former king of Jerusalem.

In 1426, an event occurred that had serious, if unforeseen, consequences down to the present day. In retaliation for raids by Cypriot pirates into their sultan's lands, the Mamelukes, the military elite of Egypt, invaded the island. In collaboration with the Genoese, who had established an enclave at Famagusta, the Mamelukes indulged in an orgy of looting, captured the king, Janus, and withdrew, their task accomplished. The *paroikoi* (serfs) took the opportunity to rebel and establish a revolutionary government. They elected a king, "Red Alexis," who organized a people's army and started executing nobles.

The rebellion was suppressed, and Red Alexis hanged May 12, 1427. This was the day King Janus landed at Paphos. The Mamelukes had released him after he paid a ransom and promised an annual tribute as a guarantee against future pirate raids by Cypriots.

In 1460, James of Lusignan, bastard son of John II, usurped the throne from his sister and her husband. James secured Venetian backing for his coup and the hand of Caterina Cornaro della Ca' Grande, whose mother's grandfather was John Comnenus, emperor of Trebizond.

Caterina, the daughter of Marco Cornaro, a friend of James, soon lost her husband and her infant son, who reigned for a year as James III and was maintained as a puppet by her countrymen. Despised by the Venetians and hated by the Cypriots, she was permitted to exist as a figurehead until the discovery of a plot in 1488 to marry her to Alfonso of Naples.

Venice formally annexed Cyprus, forced Caterina's abdication, and granted her the tiny hill town of Asolo in the Veneto region of northern Italy. There she reigned over a fantasy court until shortly before her death in Venice in 1510, where she had fled to escape the advance of Emperor Maximilian's armies.

However strict they were about their home government, Venetian rule of Cyprus was far from exemplary. Some historians blame this on the general atmosphere of corruption that allegedly pervaded the island.

Whatever the reason, bad government and an anachronistic economic and political system gave the native people an incentive to look for relief from the worst possible source. This happened to be the Ottoman Empire. . . .

THE LOGIC OF CONQUEST

Pity the Ottoman sultan Selim II, known to history as "Selim the Drunk."

Life in the shadow of a successful predecessor is never easy. When that father is Süleymân the Magnificent, it is almost impossible.

Süleymân had made a name for himself early in his reign when, almost as his first act, he took over the invasion of Rhodes planned by *his* father, Selim I, "the Grim," who had died before carrying out the self-imposed task. Süleymân assembled one of the largest armadas ever gathered together up to that time.

After a titanic struggle against the military order later known as the "Knights of Malta," when they finally found another home, Süleymân conquered Rhodes. Now, early in his own reign, Selim II set his sights on the strategically placed island of Cyprus, practically on the doorstep of the Ottoman Empire and an obvious target for acquisition.

Not that the matter was entirely the sultan's own idea, or that of Sokolli, the extremely able grand vizier he had inherited from his father and who had helped Selim to the throne. Probably intimidated by Sokolli, the profoundly indecisive Selim preferred the much more flattering attentions of Joseph Micas, "The Great Jew."

Micas, an immensely wealthy banker, had secured his position during Süleymân's reign by supplying Selim with forbidden liquor and—after playing on his fears of being poisoned—sending him sealed hampers of food he could safely eat. On ascending the throne, Selim had created Micas duke of Naxos after sending the rightful holder of the fief into exile. Now the sultan had made humorous half-promises that he would not mind seeing Micas king of Cyprus.

This worried Sokolli, fully aware that Turkish sea power depended on keeping Spain and Venice at odds. Threatening Cyprus, a key link in the Venetian trading empire, would immediately drive Venice away from France and into Spain's camp. The grand vizier also knew of Micas's habit of sacrificing the long-term good of the Ottoman Empire to gain some private end or even personal revenge—and that Micas hated the Venetians for sequestering some of his wife's property after he openly avowed Judaism.

Still, the situation seemed ideal. For one thing, Cyprus was so close to Istanbul that the supply problems that had dogged the campaigns of Süleymân the Magnificent on land and sea should practically vanish.

There was also the fact that the Greek Cypriots, of the Orthodox Christian tradition, felt themselves oppressed by their Venetian rulers, who were Latin Rite Christians. One popular leader, a teacher by the name of James Diassorinos (or Didascalos), had even been in secret communication with the Turks until he was discovered and executed in August 1562.

There was more than a little reason for this discontent. Cyprus, according to reports made to the Senate of Venice, was traditionally misgoverned. The near-stellar exception to this general rule, Senator Marcantonio Bragadino, an unusually popular governor, was only in charge of the unimportant town of Famagusta. The sultan had every reason to persuade himself of the truth of reports that fifty thousand *paroikoi* (serfs) were ready to rise in support of an Ottoman invasion.

The quality of the general run of the Venetian rectors of the island may be judged by their reaction to the Senate's instructions to emancipate the *paroikoi*, orders that were given with the full consent of the serfs' owners. This move would presumably forestall a rising and gain recruits for the defense of the island.

Instead of leaping at the chance to gain an army of partisans to harass the enemies' rear and make their lives generally miserable, the Venetian governors—with the exception, of course, of Bragadino—opposed it. Adding insult to injury, until the last minute they even forbade the relatively few Cypriots willing to fight in the island's defense to do so.

Consequently, most of the people, rich or poor, felt they had no choice but to side with the Turks, or at least stand off and avoid committing themselves. At Rhodes, the participation of the natives in the defense had made all the difference between a conquest and a negotiated surrender, while on Malta, the coordinated efforts of the Knights of the Order and the Maltese ensured a victory.

Perhaps most important, however, the Greek and Latin Churches were in conflict.

Despite the best efforts of churchmen on both sides, who saw few differences that could not easily be handled with a little goodwill, the Venetian governors felt it in their best interest to favor the Latin Rite over the Greek. The four Greek bishops were relegated to living outside the cities. In retaliation, the construction of Latin Rite churches was impeded in the countryside and Western priests were forbidden to celebrate Mass in a Greek church on anything other than a portable altar.

Then there was the fact that the armies of Sultan Selim II were badly in need of a morale boost. They had suffered two disastrous campaigns in a row, Malta and Szigetvár, lost their greatest sultan, and gained an uncontrollable alcoholic in his place.

On top of that, the war against the Persian Shia heretics had gone badly. At the same time, revolts in Syria and Yemen—Ottoman rule was not universally acceptable throughout the realm of faith—were disrupting the silk and spice trade at a cost of two million gold ducats annually. The cotton, sugar, and wine of Cyprus would be a welcome addition to the imperial revenue.

Consequently, the omens could not be better—for the sultan—whatever the wily Sokolli might say in disparagement. A son coincidentally named Selim was following a successful father, a naval operation was involved . . . and there was that delicious wine of Cyprus to reward the sultan for the inevitable victory of the invincible Ottoman armies. Of course, there was the small matter of legal claim. There was also the fact that Venice was making Selim an annual payment of nearly a quarter of a million ducats in gold annually for the privilege of trading with the Ottoman Empire . . . an arrangement that earned Venice the sobriquet "the Turkish Whore." It appeared that the only lawful course of action left open to the commander of the faithful was to wait until the agreement with the Venetians expired and refuse to renew it.

That, however, was unacceptable. Selim consulted the Mufti, the authority on interpreting the Quran. After much thought (and, no doubt, prodding from the sultan), the Mufti decided that Cyprus was legally the possession of the Ottoman Empire.

Convoluted, not to say shaky, best describes the reasoning. The justification was to be the Mameluke incursion of 1426, undertaken in retaliation for Cypriot pirate raids. This had ended with the payment of tribute as a surety against future pirate raids.

Ingeniously, the Mufti decided that the tribute (which was no longer paid!) should be reinterpreted as the submission of Cyprus to the rule of the sultan of Egypt. By stretching the point far past breaking, this meant whoever ruled Egypt rightfully ruled Cyprus.

Since Selim II's grandfather, Selim the Grim, had conquered Egypt, the present sultan was therefore the lawful ruler of Cyprus. Violating natural law (freedom of association and contract), the Mufti issued a *fatwa* that any land once belonging to Islam could be recovered by force. Any mere agreement standing in the way of such a holy objective was null and void.

Selim sent an embassy to Pietro Loredano, the venerable doge of Venice, to deliver his ultimatum: surrender Cyprus or face annihilation. In an audience on March 16, 1570, lasting less than a quarter of an hour, Loredano coldly informed the Turkish ambassador that the republic would fight.

In the meantime, the situation in Istanbul had not remained static. Sokolli, although doubtful of the wisdom of the coming campaign, had done his best to ensure its success, albeit on his terms. This would solidify his ascendancy over the others of Selim's faction who under Sokolli's leadership had helped put the sultan on the throne, Joseph Micas, Piali Pasha, and Lala Mustapha. Sokolli himself handled all the logistics, but kept his name in the background.

As far as Sokolli was concerned, this was all to the good. Micas no longer enjoyed the full confidence of the mercurial sultan or (perhaps more importantly) the bazaar mob. Always suspicious of the Great Jew's religion, the market rabble began circulating rumors that Selim was not legitimate. Explaining—so they thought—the sultan's favoring a non-Muslim and his addiction to the bottle, malcontents declared that Selim was really the son of a Jewess. Adding this to the fact that Micas stood to profit personally from a successful invasion (or so he thought) ensured that he would not be permitted to take an active role in the operation, thereby reestablishing his popularity with the people.

Nor was Piali Pasha in particularly good odor. He had tried to redeem his failure at Malta by sacking Chios, where the Genoese maintained a trading post. The operation was a success, but Piali was subsequently suspected of diverting some of the loot into his own coffers. Lala Mustapha's competence as a military commander was also questionable. He had failed spectacularly to put down the revolt in Yemen. He desperately needed something that would restore him to the sultan's favor, and take Sokolli down a peg or two. He was given co-command of the Cyprus invasion with Piali Pasha.

Sokolli had a win-win situation. If anything went wrong, one or all of the other three would take the blame. If the invasion succeeded, Sokolli stood a good chance of coming out on top. No matter what happened, Sokolli had a very good chance of being able to watch his rivals destroy themselves and still gain Cyprus for his master.

In this, Sokolli was helped more than he knew by the stupidity of Nicolò Dandolo, acting lieutenant-governor of Cyprus. Informed by the Venetian Senate of the decision to fight, Dandolo somehow reinterpreted the order to prepare for the Ottoman invasion as a signal that the real negotiations would now begin.

Astore Baglione, general of the militia, was an intelligent and efficient officer. Despite opposition and interference from Dandolo, he devoted himself to completing the defenses of Nicosia as best he could.

Baglione also advocated opposing the Turks on the coast, attacking them during their landing when there was the best chance to inflict great damage at much less risk than otherwise. Dandolo overruled him, so Baglione left Nicosia and went to Famagusta with his militia, where he got all the cooperation possible from Bragadino.

By the time the Turkish fleet under the command of Piali Pasha was sighted off the west coast on July 1, 1570, Dandolo had made no additional preparations for defense. He had even failed to stock Nicosia for a siege.

The garrison of the tiny fortress of Kyrenia, a small port on the north side of the island, was left to its own devices. Defenses of Kyrenia consisted primarily of three rebuilt towers better able to withstand cannon than the antiquated Norman keeps (a fourth of which was left standing) they had replaced soon after the Venetians took over the island.

The Turks landed at Limissò on the west coast and took a large number of the residents as slaves. The following day, July 2, the fleet set sail for the Salines, a port and town in the south that has the best harbor in the island.

Being too far from Nicosia to obtain support or reinforcements, the small troop of cavalry at the Salines under the command of the Count of Roccas offered no resistance but retired to Nicosia. Lala Mustapha unloaded all his men and equipment on July 3 and proceeded to secure his base. Reconnoitering parties met with no resistance. Local natives, probably feeling the writing was on the wall, voluntarily provided food and other supplies.

As the port facilities were in poor shape, Lala Mustapha ordered repairs made, then sent Piali Pasha back for the rest of the expeditionary force. Piali returned on July 22, and Lala Mustapha began his advance on Nicosia the next day with a force estimated at four thousand cavalry, six thousand janissaries, between twenty-five hundred and four thousand *sipahis*, and up to thirty thousand infantry, irregulars, and volunteers. Ordnance consisted of an estimated thirty heavy siege guns and fifty smaller pieces of artillery.

As the Turks expected at any moment to be set on by bands of partisans, progress was slow. They had trouble believing that no resistance was being offered and suspected a trick, so they sent out the cavalry to reconnoiter the route.

The main Turkish army arrived at Nicosia on July 25 and invested the city, establishing their camp on the southeast side. The cavalry, except for five hundred that were detached to attack Famagusta, arrived the next day. No surviving records relate what happened to the troopers that went to Famagusta, but it can be assumed that they returned when they saw that preparations for the defense of that town were well advanced.

Once his forces were all gathered together before Nicosia, Lala Mustapha had his *sipahis* ride up to the walls of the city and challenge the defenders to come out and fight. They refused. Given the weakness of the defenders, this made more than a little sense.

The Turks settled down to carry on a more conventional siege and began constructing forts and digging zigzag trenches around the perimeter of the city. While not very effective, the forts were used as bases from which to bombard the walls. As the trenches could not be enfiladed (fire directed at the longest axis of the trenches) from the ramparts of the town, the defenders returned equally ineffective fire.

The initial Turkish bombardment lasted for four days, from first light to dark, pausing only during the heat of midday for the gunners to rest and let the guns cool. Most of the shells never hit the walls of the city but buried themselves uselessly in the earthen ramparts that constituted the greater part of the defenses.

Under cover of the zigzag trenches, Lala Mustapha then set up a second line of batteries closer to the walls and had the engineers—meaning large numbers of slave laborers—begin digging long, deep trenches straight toward the city's earthworks. The defenders countered with artillery fire, putting a number of Turkish guns out of action.

Despite their losses, the Ottoman attack moved slowly forward. They dug a trench opposite the counterscarp (the outer side of the city's defensive ditch), from which their harquebusiers kept up a continuous fire day and night against anyone who appeared on the walls.

The Turks also surrounded their trenches and fortified strongpoints with ditches and large, deep excavations. These served not only to hide large bodies of men from the defenders but also prevented the Nicosians from making any effective sallies to destroy the enemy siege works without great loss.

Great trenches dug by the Turkish engineers soon penetrated the city's defensive outer ditch. Once in, they threw up their own earthworks on the flanks. This gave the Turks cover from which to attack and begin to demolish the four outer bastions or strongpoints on the south side of the city walls. They began filling in the trenches with earth and bundles of brush to prevent a counterattack and ready the ground for an assault once the walls were breached.

Seeing this, the defenders made a sally on August 15. This was carefully timed for midday, when the Turks were resting and avoiding the heat.

A thousand Italian and Cypriot infantrymen under the command of Captain Piovene of Vicenza attacked the Turkish outposts and captured two of the forts. Taken by surprise, the Turks retreated in a panic.

Unfortunately, the defenders' cavalry failed to come out as planned to support the infantry attack. This gave the *sipahis*, the Turkish cavalry, time to regroup and counter-attack. Piovene and another captain were killed, along with about a hundred soldiers.

The Nicosians retreated, bringing back a little loot but accomplishing nothing. As the cost was too great, no further attempts were made to harass the Turks, and operations became purely defensive.

Two of the bastions on the south side were transformed into redoubts (small fortified areas) by closing off most of the access from the city, the "throats." This created a place to which the defenders could retreat without giving any foothold to the attackers.

This, however, was only temporary, as it could not prevent the Turks from continuing to construct ramps by means of which they were able to attack up to all four bastions of the walls at once. These attacks were beaten off, but at great cost on both sides, including "great waste of rockets and other fireworks," according to the eyewitness account of Giovanni Pietro Contarini, who wrote a general history of the entire war up to the battle of Lepanto.

Becoming desperate, the defenders sent a plea to Famagusta for reinforcements. The first messengers were captured and paraded before the eyes of the Nicosians. Captain Giovanni Battista Columba, "a man of weight and resource," as Contarini called him, then volunteered to try.

He was able to reach Famagusta and return, but no aid was forthcoming from that quarter. They then sent messengers to the Cypriots in the hills, but these, too, were captured. To bring the matter to a swift conclusion, on September 8, Lala Mustapha requested additional troops from the base at the Salines. A hundred men were landed from each galley, and the twenty thousand reinforcements reached Nicosia by forced march by 10 p.m. the same day, where Lala Mustapha greeted them "with great joy and all honor."

At dawn the next morning, Sunday, September 9, the Turks launched a final offensive on all four bastions simultaneously.

The first assaults were beaten off "with fierce slaughter on both sides," although—as is usual in such situations—with greater losses among the attackers. None of the enemy was able to get over the parapet, the low wall at the top of the defensive perimeter.

With the aid of the reinforcements from the galleys, however—of which the defenders knew nothing—the Turks were able to keep up the pressure. They were finally able to penetrate one of the bastions and overwhelm the platform and the redoubt.

Most of the professional soldiers and officers died at their posts. Some of the Cypriot irregulars managed to get out through the embrasures or by lowering themselves down the curtain wall and saved themselves by running away.

Alerted by the noise and confusion of the attack, a number of officers and gentleman volunteers with a few soldiers in support rushed to reinforce the position. For a brief time they managed to drive the Turks back but were soon overcome by sheer force of numbers. Every one of them died fighting.

The Turks poured into the city. Soldiers and nobles who attempted to stand and fight were surrounded and slaughtered, as were any townsmen found. Fighting ranged through every street and square in the city. Anyone who defended himself or was caught in the blood-frenzy that seems inevitable when a town is taken by storm was killed. Anyone who surrendered was taken prisoner and enslaved.

Total confusion reigned, and the massacre continued until about noon. Some few soldiers and townsmen managed to make their way to the three surviving bastions, which held out until the very end. Finally, however, they were taken from the rear, through the "throats" that connected them to the city, which were poorly defended against an attack coming from that quarter.

Finally, Lala Mustapha entered the city and ordered his soldiers to stop fighting. He guaranteed the lives of anyone who surrendered. A few took his offer and were immediately enslaved. Most refused and died fighting.

On hearing the news of the fall of Nicosia, the commander of Kyrenia surrendered. Soon after, the rest of the island capitulated, with the exception of Famagusta.

The reinforcements from the galleys made their way back to the Salines. Lala Mustapha garrisoned Nicosia with four thousand infantry and one thousand cavalry and began the advance on Famagusta.

HISTORICAL NOTE: "A LITTLE OF THE '71"

The annals of war give many and varied reasons for invading another country: manifest destiny, racial imperative, religion, economics, even politics. The 1570–71 invasion of Cyprus, however, is one of the oddest, at least according to some historians. Legend has it that the sultan Selim the Drunk targeted the island for takeover by the Muslim Ottomans, teetotal by Islamic law, because he wanted a drink.

The island of Cyprus has been famed since ancient times for its fine wine. In the eighteenth century, an Italian priest, the Abbé Giovanni Mariti, in his unique chronicle of Cyprus, *Viaggi per l'isola di Cipro* (1769), described the production of the various types and the market in some detail. The good father even credited it as being an effective cure for a fever that sounds suspiciously like malaria, but which the observant reverend gentleman was certain had another cause than mere "bad air," although mere insect bites were, of course, not considered.

Selim II was son and successor to the sultan known in the West as Süleymân the Magnificent and to the Turks as *Qanani*, "the Lawgiver." According to Turkish theory, the sultan was technically the owner of everyone and everything that existed, the slave master and universal proprietor of the world.

Selim, however, was himself a slave to alcohol. His favorite tipple was the wine of Cyprus. Naturally, since he felt he legally owned the island and its people anyway, why not take possession and ensure his source of supply? Thus—so the story goes—he ordered the conquest of Cyprus.

After the sieges, despite the heroic resistance offered to the Turkish invasion by the bishops and monks in Nicosia and the citizens of Famagusta under the leadership of a popular leader named Marmaras, the people of the countryside in general felt they had no other choice than to side with the Turks. For their assistance, they were promised freedom of religion and a number of political and social benefits, such as emancipation for the serfs, which—in something of a surprise twist—had been proposed earlier by their owners but denied by the Venetian overlords.

Unfortunately, after the Turks captured the island, the benefits lasted only a couple of years before the native population found their new lot harder than the old. While many histories maintain that the Greek Church, freed from the oppression of the pope, flourished under the Ottomans, that was only true officially.

The upper classes either "Muslimized" or changed from Latin to Orthodox Christianity. They not only retained their old habits of oppression but added Turkish features. Taxes went up (this was the direct cause of the Insurrection of 1764 when both Greeks and Turks rose up against the imperial governor who was lining his own pockets by doubling the legal taxes), usury was prevalent, and religious practice for both Latin and Orthodox Christians, unless you happened to be a member of the favored classes, was threatened and discouraged. The situation was almost exactly analogous to that which prevailed in Sicily, with similar results reaching down to the present day.

Still, Selim the Drunk got his wine. According to some sources, he had satisfied tradition by adding Cyprus to the empire and took little interest in warfare after that.

Of course, the stunning defeat at Lepanto a few months later might also have had something to do with the sultan's disinterest in public policy matters and expanding the empire by conquest. He retired to his harem and his bottle and died "worn out" from indulging in pleasure in December 1574.

Others maintain that Selim met his end in an even more ignoble fashion. He got drunk and slipped in the bath, suffering a skull fracture that ended his life in a delirium a few days later.

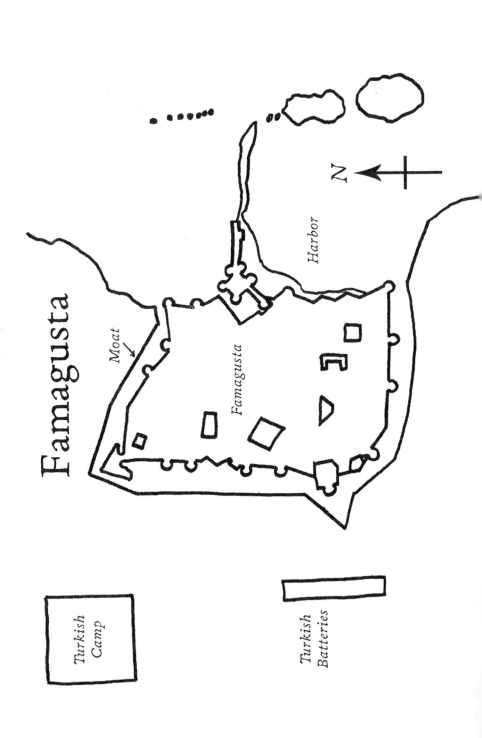

Famagusta

Turkish
Camp

Turkish
Batteries

Moat

Famagusta

Harbor

N

9

FAMAGUSTA

1570–71

IT was a glorious day in the annals of the armies of the Prophet. The city of Nicosia, the capital of Cyprus, had fallen to the forces of the sultan on September 9, 1570, after a siege of forty-six days. The surrender of the five hundred Venetians remaining in their final stronghold of the governor's palace under the command of Nicolò Dandolo had been accepted.

In celebration, the prisoners had been slaughtered to a man and the twenty thousand inhabitants of the city put to the sword—those not deemed worthy to offer on the slave blocks of Istanbul. Specifics of how the townspeople were put to death are usually considered too obscene to relate.

The capitulation of Nicosia almost made up for the disaster at Malta a few years before, at least in terms of morale. It demonstrated once again the invincibility of an Islamic army when fighting under the sacred green banner of the Prophet.

Only two things marred the day. After the two thousand carefully selected boys and girls were herded off to end up in the brothels and harems of Istanbul, a young woman by the name of Amalda de Rocas managed to make her way to the powder magazine of a vessel belonging to Sokolli, the Ottoman grand vizier. She blew the ship, the cargo of plunder, and eight hundred slaves to kingdom come.

The other irritant was the failure of the defenders of the ancient town and crusader castle of Famagusta to surrender instantly. . . .

THE MARTYRDOM OF BRAGADINO

The unconquerable armies of the Ottoman Empire, now under the command (indirectly) of Süleymân's son, Selim II, were at the gates of the city of Famagusta. They were demanding the immediate and unconditional surrender of the Venetian garrison and city administration.

The offer was made in traditional fashion. Turkish *sipahis*—cavalry—had ridden the fifty kilometers cross country that separated Famagusta from Nicosia with the heads of Nicolò Dandolo and other town fathers and leaders of the latter city decorating the tips of their lances.

They found the port city of Famagusta and the old castle manned by seven thousand defenders under the command of the civil governor Marcantonio Bragadino and his military counterpart, Astor Baglione, general of the militia. Neither of these was willing to listen to any offers of surrender—especially with the evidence of Turkish clemency staring them in the face. These were men of the caliber of the defenders of Malta and of Szigetvár and not likely to give in easily in any event, even if they had not had the example of the earlier heroes constantly before them.

The tiny harbor of Famagusta was perfectly situated for defense; the castle overlooked the anchorage and was able to protect any vessels in range of its guns. An iron chain closed the harbor in time of war, effective even against the shallow-draft galleys that formed the backbone of naval power in the Mediterranean. Northward ranged Cape San Andrea with Cape Greca to the west, providing shelter and additional defense at the same time.

The civil defenses consisted of a parapet a little over a meter high positioned at the crest of an earthen rampart. The walls were each just short of a kilometer long, punctuated with small defensive towers.

While the siege of Nicosia progressed, Bragadino and Baglione had made good use of the time so dearly bought. Instead of wasting resources on a futile attempt to relieve the capital, efforts were redoubled to strengthen their town's rather feeble defenses.

The suburbs, the sections of the town outside the walls, were razed to give a clear field of fire. An effort was made to remove non-combatants from the area. By the end of the siege, approximately eight thousand had been relocated, presumably out of harm's way.

Becoming less than convinced that the Turks would be better than the Venetians, however, several hundred Greek Orthodox Cypriots volunteered to help the usually detested Latin Rite Catholics defend the town. When the Turkish *sipahis* rode up with the grisly burdens on the ends of their lances, the tiny city was about as well prepared as could be expected to resist the enemy.

In view of this unaccountable stubbornness and resistance to the inevitable, Lala Mustapha, commander of the Islamic land forces, surrounded the tiny city with batteries of siege artillery—twenty-five cannon directed against the rather insubstantial western wall alone. These commenced a regular bombardment almost immediately.

It was now, however, too late in the year to begin siege operations. Any day, the Mediterranean could become stormy and virtually impassable for supply ships. The port was blockaded with seven galleys, and the Turkish forces that remained in the field went into winter quarters on Cape Creca.

The rest of the Ottoman fleet made its way through unseasonably rough seas to bases in the Dardenelles, Rhodes, Chios, and Negropont. Much to Sultan Selim's alcohol-soaked rage, the summer campaign of 1570 had ground to a halt.

Selim nearly went berserk. Impatient for a victory, he dismissed Piali Pasha from command of the fleet. The commander of the faithful insisted that it was Piali's fault that the Venetian naval forces were able to move about with such ease.

It was not—it was merely that the Turks had been unable to engage the Venetians in battle. The Italian fleet had been too slow to engage when they could have, and the supremely cautious Admiral Marcantonio Colonna was not about to risk ships and men to assuage public opinion.

Only the fact that he was married to one of Selim's daughters saved Piali Pasha from the block or worse. Not that it would have displeased Grand Vizier Sokolli if his rival had been put to death.

Just because the Cypriot campaign was going nowhere did not mean that the invaders could relax, however. Two brothers of the House of Rondacchi were in command of the town's small troop of cavalry. They got into the habit of making frequent bold sallies across the ramparts and into the heart of the besieging force.

Raiding parties went out from the city against the Turkish batteries swinging hand grenades that wreaked havoc among the enemy gunners. Throughout the winter, a native workforce was kept continually at work, piling the earthen ramparts higher against the inevitable storming of the city.

One feat that seems incredible even to read about was the counter to a mine the Turkish sappers dug through solid rock under the wall—an amazing accomplishment of its own. Nestor Martinengo, Bragadino's chief sapper and artillery commander, responded in classic fashion. He had a countermine dug under the Turkish mine in approved fashion.

Famagusta was, however, short of powder. The defenders had none to waste on exploding an enemy mine prematurely, even if the rulebook demanded that course of action.

Instead, the Venetians waited underneath until they heard the Turkish sappers place the barrels of powder, light the fuse, and run away. Then Martinengo's men surged up through a prepared tunnel, put out the fuse, and absconded with the Turkish explosives.

When the siege was five months old, on January 26, 1571, the Turks received a less insulting but far more demoralizing surprise.

According to some sources, the seven galleys of the Turkish blockade were beached on the shore of Constanza Bay under the cover of a friendly battery. Other pro-Turkish sources maintain that the galleys were anchored in the water.

Regardless, the vessels were pinned against the shore in an unbelievably disadvantageous position when sixteen galleys from the Venetian base at Candia on Crete appeared, escorting three armed merchantmen loaded to the gunwales with reinforcements, food, and munitions. Commanded by Marcantonio Quirini, they had made the passage from Candia to Famagusta in an astounding eight days through bad seas. Initially beached or still afloat, the Turkish galleys managed to make a run for it, but with Quirini's little flotilla in close pursuit. His merchant vessels, of course, made straight for the port, where the chain was rapidly removed in anticipation of their entry. In a quick action, Quirini sank three of the Turkish ships while the remaining four escaped under cover of darkness.

Returning to port, Quirini supervised the unloading of 1,600 reinforcements and supplies. Taking off the sick, wounded, and remaining non-combatants, he immediately set sail for a cruise around the island, leaving Luigi Martinengo in command of the new contingent. With a display of panache that infuriated the Turks, he burned watchtowers, captured and sank two huge supply ships (possibly provided as a speculation in the war by the sultan's harem, which had a habit of investing in such endeavors), and sent raiding parties ashore to disrupt communications.

The garrison was even more heartened a short time later when a blockade-runner arrived from Venice. This carried a troop of eight hundred soldiers under the command of Onorio Scotto and, more importantly in terms of morale, a personal letter of encouragement from the Venetian Senate addressed to "Our most dear and faithful city of Famagusta."

The defenders reassured themselves that the republic had not forgotten them—nor had it. In continuing negotiations with Sokolli, the Venetians insisted that, while they were willing to concede much, the garrison of Famagusta must be accorded honorable treatment.

Sokolli stated on more than one occasion that such gallant foes not only deserved decent treatment but had earned it many times over. Underestimating his rival Lala Mustapha's ambition and greed and the sultan's stupidity, and looking forward to a brilliant diplomatic coup, Sokolli gave his personal word of honor that the lives of the defenders would be held sacred in the event of a surrender.

For their part, the defenders of Famagusta, unaware that they had become *cause celebré* throughout Europe, told themselves that when the Turks renewed the offensive in the spring, the mighty fleet of the Venetian Republic would intercept the Turkish armada and destroy it. They still had not grasped the fact that the only thing the Turks held cheaper than the lives of their enemies and slaves were the lives of their own soldiers and sailors.

Only the sultan himself matched this by the incredible, even foolish, lengths to which he would go to achieve even a minor gain or satisfy an urge. Selim's father, Süleymân the Magnificent, had diverted what had been planned as the greatest campaign of his entire career, the capture of Vienna, to revenge himself for a personal insult thrown in his face by Count Myklós Zrínyi, the hero of Szigetvár.

His father's son in this if nothing else, Selim the Drunk informed his divan—his advisory council—that no military operations whatsoever were to be planned or carried out until Famagusta had been taken. Bragadino and the rest of the defenders would have been stunned had they known what Selim was planning in order to secure an unimportant city that was already nearly his by negotiations carried on by the wily Sokolli.

As far as the defenders were concerned, all they had to do was to hold out until their stubbornness put Venice into a bargaining position that would allow the Queen of the Adriatic to salvage something from certain defeat. To achieve a victory, all the Turks had to do was leave a skeleton force besieging the city as a bargaining chip and talk the Venetians into surrender. This would have freed virtually the whole of the Turkish military might to pursue the sultan's grandiose schemes.

Selim's insistence on reducing Famagusta by sheer force instead of negotiation before going on to anything else had already set back the Turkish program of conquest by at least a year. The taking of Cyprus had been planned as a glorious exhibition of Ottoman might and a demonstration of the futility of resistance to the holy armies of the Prophet.

A European might wonder at an ephemeral goal achieved at stupendous cost; the Turkish method of besieging and storming a city typically cost the attacker tens of thousands of lives. Except for rare cases like Sokolli, however, the Turks had no doubts. The Venetians had to be taught a lesson for their insolence.

It did not help any that Famagusta was to be sacrificed to satisfy Lala Mustapha's political ambitions. Lala Mustpha was fully aware that Sokolli needed a negotiated surrender that would advance his, Sokolli's, aims and hopefully satisfy the Venetians enough to keep them out of Spain's camp. Lala Mustapha also knew that his influence on the sultan, along with that of Piali Pasha and Joseph Micas, was declining.

By giving Selim what he wanted, a spectacular (and costly) victory, an order he could easily have ignored, Lala Mustapha's star would presumably rise and Sokolli's would set. The victor of Famagusta might even find himself grand vizier in Sokolli's place—or so Lala Mustapha seemed to think. Thus, the war fleets of the Turks set out to sea almost before it was feasible, launching in February of 1571. This was well before the ordinary campaigning season and at a time when there was no certainty that the weather would be suitable for sailing.

Galleys from Istanbul were joined by contingents from Rhodes, Chios, and even Egypt. Approximately two hundred vessels were collected and sent to crush all resistance at Famagusta.

Supreme command of the assembled fleet was given to Ali the Muezzin. He had previously commanded the much smaller naval contingent during the siege of Nicosia after the removal of Piali Pasha. He had risen to his present eminence by the effect his melodious voice had on the occupants of the sultan's harem as he issued the call to prayer from the minaret near the palace.

Ali took his place with the vanguard and arrived off Cyprus with seventy galleys in April. It was not long before the defenders on the walls of Famagusta observed the janissaries, *sipahis*, other troops, and auxiliaries arrive and begin pitching camp.

The Turkish host totaled perhaps as many as 250,000. Opposed to them were approximately 4,000 defenders of the weakened garrison, the pre-siege operations having taken their toll.

Of course, a great many of the men crowded around the walls of Famagusta were not combatants. The Islamic effectives probably numbered around one hundred thousand, bad enough odds considering the small number of defenders. The additional men were not just there to intimidate the Venetians, however. Turkish assault methods required tens of thousands of forced laborers to drive trenches forward before the overwhelming assault directed toward overcoming resistance by sheer mass of humanity. These often died by the thousands, for, as mentioned earlier, the Turks usually drove their trenches straight toward the walls of their target rather than "zigzag" in the European fashion to provide cover for the workers.

Lala Mustapha was still commander-in-chief of the land forces. He smirked that if each one of his soldiers simply removed one of their sandals, they would make a mound high enough to scale the walls of the city.

Probably realizing that even Turks could not fight very effectively running lopsided, however, he almost immediately set the forced labor contingents digging the necessary trenches through rock, suffering hideous casualties. Within a month and a half, the trenches were so deep that a man on horseback entering the excavation with his lance straight up could not be seen.

The Turks still attempted to sap the walls of the city. The Venetians again countermined, but this time did not bother to try and make off with the powder. They simply blew them to pieces in the approved manner. Turkish engineers attempting to drive the trenches or place additional batteries were attacked almost continuously by small parties wielding hand grenades.

Turkish losses mounted at an appalling rate. The grand mufti, however, had declared the Cyprus invasion a jihad, or holy war, although the justification for this to westerners or even other Muslims might be a little unclear—especially since the entire campaign was reportedly rooted in Selim's thirst for the famed wine of Cyprus. The attackers were thus assured, at least to some degree, that their cause was just and that they need not fear death, having won heaven simply by perishing in the endeavor of assaulting an enemy.

The iron circle around the city continued to tighten in spite of the enormous casualties. By the end of May, Lala Mustapha had managed to position no less than seventy-four cannon arranged in ten batteries opposite the weakest points in the defenses. Four of these guns were "basilisks"; that is, enormous siege weapons capable of smashing two-hundred-pound balls against the walls of the city.

Still, the makeshift defenses of Famagusta proved adequate for the time being. Although breaches were made in the earthen ramparts at regular intervals, these were quickly repaired with hundreds of sandbags thrown into the gap bucket-brigade fashion.

One morale builder not imitated by the Turkish leadership was the fact that the Venetian commanders established their headquarters in dugouts under the very walls of the city, carrying out their tasks and even eating and sleeping at the post of maximum danger. Ottoman commanders took their ease in silken pavilions well out of range of the city's guns or raiding parties.

Nevertheless, the Turkish war machine continued to grind down the city. Using the enormous trenches dug by forced labor to the best advantage, the Turks were able to construct a "bomb proof" gun emplacement under the ramparts of the city at point blank range.

The gun emplacement may have been bomb proof, but it was not audacity proof. Before it could have any material effect, the Venetians made a sally and destroyed it.

For their battle flag, the Turks were using a Venetian banner adorned with the lion of Saint Mark that had been captured at the sack of Nicosia. Nothing daunted, Astor Baglione personally led a band of men and took back the flag with his own hand.

In late June, however, the Turks finally managed to make a breach in the walls that was too big to close up. Lala Mustapha, already humiliated by the sustained fight the defenders had put up and no doubt being pressed by his own ambition and the sultan for results, ordered a simultaneous attack on all parts of the city.

To soften up the garrison and ensure maximum confusion, smudges were lit. The idea was to smoke the defenders out from behind their walls, blinded and choking.

In this, the Turks were somewhat successful, but the tactic had no effect on the outcome. By July 9, three massed attacks had been beaten back with enormous losses.

A fourth massed attack on July 31 also failed, even though the city walls were breached in six places and a bare 1,800 defenders were left alive. The Rondacchi brothers had ceased their cavalry sorties—almost all the horses had been eaten.

The garrison was almost out of flour with which to make bread. A count after the siege revealed seven barrels of gunpowder remaining. Marcantonio Bragadino, the civil governor, decided to take advice and arrange for a parley.

In spite of the horrors precipitated by this decision, it was the only reasonable, indeed, only possible thing Bragadino could have done, at least without certain knowledge of the future. Had what lay in store for him and his people been revealed by one of the ever-popular astrologers of the day, who plied their trade contrary to both canon and civil law, he might have decided differently and continued to resist.

Marcantonio Bragdino was a senator of the Venetian Republic. Although the city had gone into something of a decline, it had achieved greatness not primarily on its military might but on the strength of its negotiating skills.

As far as Bragadino knew, he held not only the moral high ground but every political advantage. In addition, Lala Mustapha was under extreme pressure from his alcoholic ruler to show some results for the huge investment of men and material.

For eleven months, the defenders had held out against an army originally outnumbering them by more than fifty to one. The Turks had better equipment, more supplies, and the imams' constant encouragement of a sure place in paradise and eternal delight in the arms of beautiful *houris* to spur them on to greater efforts.

An estimated 150,000 cannonballs were flung at the city walls, most of them after April when the siege had properly started. Even calculating over the full ten months of the siege, that works out to an average of 500 per day, at a time when loading cannon was hard work, especially a basilisk that hurled two-hundred-pound balls. In the twenty-four hours preceding the third massed assault of July 9, more than 5,000 shot were expended in a futile attempt to soften up the defenders.

Aside from the usual carnage of tens of thousands among the forced labor contingents (whom the Turks rarely counted), a minimum—*minimum*—of fifty-two thousand effectives of the original estimated one hundred thousand had perished. These had been lost in the endless attempts to take the outer, presumably weaker, defenses.

As far as Lala Mustapha knew, Bragadino could drive the cost up even further by retreating to the citadel. A similar situation at Szigetvár five years previously had cost the Turks tens of thousands of casualties to take the inner defenses held by the remaining six hundred defenders.

The clincher was the fact that the Turks had no idea whether the Senate of Venice intended to mount a campaign to relieve the city. Something was obviously in the air—Pope Pius V had been working feverishly organizing and doing . . . something. Erstwhile enemies from all over Europe were pledging men, arms, supplies, and equipment for some vast undertaking.

The puzzle for the Turks was . . . *what*? Like the German high command in the Second World War, Lala Mustapha knew that something big was coming, and that "something big" was a military campaign.

The *when* was also evident from the level of activity—sometime within the next one or two months. With the right approach—and, as a Venetian senator, Bragadino was a master of the "right approach"—the Turkish commander could easily be convinced that the *where* was Famagusta itself.

To Bragadino, it was obvious that the Senate had decided that the city was expendable. No relief was to be expected—the real *where* was to be somewhere else. Two months later, it turned out to be the Gulf of Lepanto, with the *what* being the almost complete destruction of the Turkish navy. The Turks could not be expected to know that, however.

According to the laws of war, a city that surrendered after parley was granted the lives and property of its citizens. The garrison was allowed to go free, usually carrying away its personal weapons.

The presumed end result of a negotiated surrender was a simple change in government. Nicosia had been taken by storm, which fact, somewhat understandably given the state of mind of attackers in the heat of battle, would at least explain the massacre of the garrison and the slaughter and enslavement of the citizens.

There could be no such excuse in the case of Famagusta. By all the signs, Bragadino was in the best possible bargaining position—a win-win situation. After a series of secret negotiations, the city was yielded to the Turks on August 1, 1571.

All things considered, Bragadino had secured a very favorable bargain. Life and liberty were granted to everyone within the walls of the besieged city. Citizens could go or stay. If they chose to stay, their property and freedom of religion were guaranteed.

The garrison was to be allowed to march out with full honors of war, retaining their personal weapons and five pieces of artillery. The three principal commanders were to be allowed to ride out of the city on horseback—a noble rather than a dishonorable exit.

Forty Turkish galleys were designated to carry the garrison and any citizens who chose to leave to Crete, at that time still in the hands of the Venetian Republic. By August 1, the sick and wounded had actually been moved on to the galleys. To all appearances, Marcantonio Bragadino had achieved a brilliant diplomatic success following a remarkable military campaign.

Appearances, however, can be deceiving. Lala Mustapha appears at this point to have gone almost insane, a judgment borne out by subsequent events. The only possible explanation is that, having expended enormous resources to achieve the military victory the sultan demanded, all Lala Mustapha had accomplished was what Sokolli had originally proposed months before, which only made the grand vizier look that much better.

On August 4, Lala Mustapha summoned Bragadino and his chief officers to his tent for an additional parley. For four days everything had run smoothly, and the civil governor's demeanor was such that he clearly suspected nothing.

After a cordial greeting and opening, however, Mustapha seemed to lose his mind. Modern historians still debate whether the emotions he displayed were real or feigned, but the results were the same.

First, the Turkish commander accused Bragadino of executing prisoners of war during the truce. He then demanded sureties for the galleys assigned to carry the garrison away to Crete.

Bragadino, an experienced politician, probably realized instantly that Mustapha was seeking some pretext to break or modify the agreement, although the Turk's actual plans would have revolted him. The Venetian responded with calm dignity that these issues should have been raised during the negotiation process.

Bragadino's failure to take the bait infuriated the Turk. Lala Mustapha then changed tactics in an attempt to find something that would be sufficiently insulting or degrading to put the onus of bad faith on Bragadino. His eyes fell on Bragadino's page, a young boy named Antonio Quirini, who had managed to escape from the butchery at Nicosia although his father had been one of the victims of the atrocity.

The Turkish commander hinted rather broadly to Bragadino that the young man would make a splendid addition to the Turkish commander's bed and demanded the person of the young page as hostage for the safe return of the forty galleys. Bragadino mildly replied that there was nothing in the agreement about hostages.

Tired of trying to manufacture a pretext, Lala Mustapha then gave a signal to his guards. It is one of the great ironies of history that the subsequent acts of the Turkish commander-in-chief, designed to demonstrate Ottoman invincibility, were to inspire the Venetians at Lepanto to achieve victory at any cost.

The guards dragged the governor and his companions out of Lala Mustapha's tent and put Bragadino immediately into chains. Astor Baglione and the other men of the party were hacked to pieces before Bragadino's eyes, the executioners apparently taking great care that a large measure of the blood of his friends and compatriots splattered the governor.

The only survivors apart from Bragadino were a couple of pages to whom the Turks had taken a fancy, and who were to survive the horrors of a Turkish captivity to tell the tale later. As an example of Turkish humor, Bragadino was forced to the headsman's block three times "to test his courage." Instead of his head, however, they cut off his nose and both ears—one at a time.

Back in Famagusta, Tiepolo, the subordinate in charge, had no idea what was going on. For all he knew, everything was proceeding according to Bragadino's agreement rather than Lala Mustapha's plan.

The garrison was marched down to the galleys and went to their assigned places. Once there, however, the Turks seized the soldiers, stripped them, and chained them to oars. Tiepolo was hanged.

Bragadino's wounds were carefully tended to ensure sport at a future time. Two weeks later, Friday, August 17, 1571 (the Muslim holy day), Bragadino was harnessed like an animal, loaded with rocks, and driven on his hands and knees past the Turkish gun emplacements where he was pelted with filth. Whenever he was led in front of Lala Mustapha's tent, the dignified old senator was forced to kiss the dirt.

The Turks now drew up the galleys in which the garrison had been chained as slaves so that the Venetians could share in the entertainment. That portion of the show consisted merely of hoisting up the hapless governor at a rope's end in a chair so that his erstwhile comrades in arms could view his mutilated condition.

From the ships, Bragadino was moved to the city and put in the stocks to impress the Greek citizens. Witnesses later said that he remained calm throughout the ordeal, only breaking his composure to pray in Latin.

Lala Mustapha then had a private showing in which, the Turkish commander licking his lips in anticipation, Bragadino was skinned alive, starting with the feet. He died before the completion of the process, when the executioner had only gotten waist high.

Continuing the disgusting farce, Bragadino's skin was tanned and stuffed with straw. This hideous manikin was taken through the streets of the city with all the honors traditionally shown to a Venetian senator and attached to the yardarm of Lala Mustapha's personal galley, along with the heads of Luigi Martinengo and Giovanni Antonio Quirini, two military commanders during the siege.

Upon arrival in Istanbul, the remains were paraded through the streets in a bizarre parody of a Roman triumph. After that, what was left of Bragadino's body was incarcerated in a slave prison.

Turkish honor was satisfied. The siege of Famagusta was over.

HISTORICAL NOTE: COLLABORATION OR ACCOMMODATION?

Why did the countries of eastern Europe fail to participate to what others considered the proper extent in the wars against the Turks? Presumably opposed ideologically as well as religiously and politically to the menace at their very doorstep, why was there such a high incidence along the border marches of alliance, subordination, and, on occasion, active participation in wars on the side of the enemies of Christendom? At times it seemed very close to outright treason against the remnants of Roman civilization, especially when the fall of Constantinople removed the West's strongest bastion against Turkish imperialism.

Primary blame for the accommodation is geographical. The Islamic sphere of influence in general had been on the European doorstep for eight centuries. And that doorstep is eastern Europe. With the Turks continually attempting invasions to conquer the rest of Europe, the danger was constant, except when the sultan's interest happened to shift temporarily somewhere else.

The border marches especially were often composed of Christian peoples ruled by Muslim overlords. They were thus in a constant state of ferment. Sometimes, as in nominally tributary Wallachia under Vlad III (Dracula), the local people were able to throw off the Turkish yoke temporarily. Vlad, for example, is credited with being the only man ever to frighten the infamous Sultan Mehmet II, conqueror of Constantinople.

As in Spain, however, where Christians and Moors found it to their advantage at times to get along and even cooperate to some extent, local rulers on both sides in eastern Europe would form temporary alliances with each other. Tartar light cavalry fought on the side of Poland and Lithuania in the great battle of Tannenburg in 1410, while Cossacks and various European mercenaries were often able to gain employment with the Turks in their unending battles against other Islamic powers.

The incidence of either Turks or Europeans joining with the other side against members of their own respective faiths, however, appears to have been extremely low. Still, when such renegades appeared, their effectiveness and ferocity was often all out of proportion to what might otherwise be expected.

It was generally the case that when either a Christian or a Muslim turned against his own faith, there was some personal grudge involved. It rarely had anything to do with religious tenets.

Ochiali—El Louck Ali—for example, a criminal turned Turkish admiral, had a psychotic hatred of Catholic and Orthodox priests. After his capture by the Turks and a short stint as a galley slave, he had no hesitation in becoming Muslim by uttering the *inshallah*. The Turks were glad to use him against his erstwhile co-religionists, but never really trusted him.

The question then becomes not why the peoples of eastern Europe failed to participate to a greater degree against the Turks. Rather, the question is why central and western European support for their fellow Christians to the east was so sporadic.

Eastern Europe suffered from continual warfare for eight centuries. Naturally, their participation in the occasional Crusades or counterattacks from the West would be "low." They were already engaged in the war.

Spain's participation in the various Crusades was equally small. They were already fighting the war and could spare nothing. Had the peoples of eastern Europe contributed in any significant measure to the usual Western type of response, they would have stripped themselves of their defenses and left both themselves and the West wide open to any determined Turkish campaign.

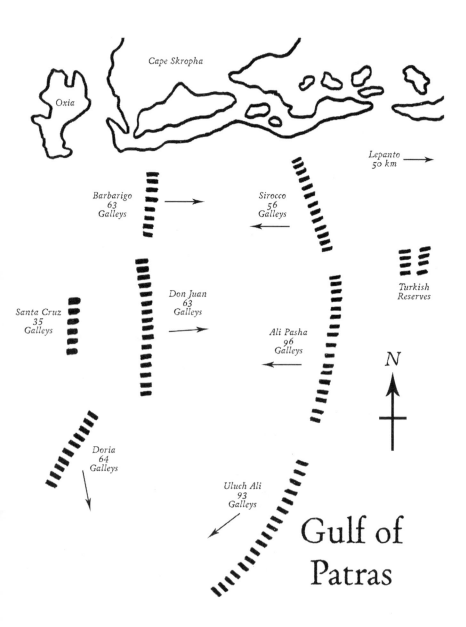

Cape Skropha

Oxia

Lepanto
50 km →

Barbarigo
63
Galleys

Sirocco
56
Galleys

Turkish
Reserves

Santa Cruz
35
Galleys

Don Juan
63
Galleys

Ali Pasha
96
Galleys

N

Doria
64
Galleys

Uluch Ali
93
Galleys

Gulf of
Patras

10

LEPANTO I

1571

THE modern cynic sneers and wonders what the fuss was about. The people of the sixteenth century, however, had no doubt at all about the importance of the battle of Lepanto on October 7, 1571. At stake was the survival of Western civilization. Descriptions of the situation and the battle bear a strong resemblance to Armageddon, the final conflict between good and evil.

Although the threat of the Grand Turk would continue for a few centuries more, the battle that day marked the apex of Ottoman power in the Mediterranean. From that fateful day in the final third of the sixteenth century, the menace would be contained, although the West could never rest easy. At the moment, however, everything hung in the balance.

Until then, the Turks could claim, with some degree of truth, never to have been defeated in battle. They had withdrawn and retreated, but a specific defeat, never . . . depending, of course, on how one happened to define *defeat*.

All that, however, was in the past. The Grand Turk was out for revenge.

In addition, the empire needed some showy triumph to make up for a series of costly victories and near-conquests. Selim II, a life-long alcoholic, wanted revenge for his father's failed siege of Malta and for the sacrifice of the defenders of the castle of Szigetvár that had derailed Süleymân the Magnificent's planned final assault on Vienna. Most especially, Selim wanted heavy payment for the successful but costly and completely unnecessary siege of Famagusta—and he meant to have it. There was also the incentive that each Ottoman ruler was expected to add to the empire and the sphere of Islam by conquest.

Selim had managed to take Cyprus, an island to which the Turks had manufactured a somewhat tenuous claim to justify breaking a treaty with Venice. A great victory at sea would not merely follow up on the momentum of the Cyprus campaign, it would allow the despised Selim the Drunk to do what his great father had never been able to accomplish: open the gateway for the conquest of Europe.

All he had to do was win. . . .

"THAT PRODIGIOUS BATTLE"

The Ottoman fleet moved slowly toward the ships of the Holy League. Arrayed more or less in a giant crescent, the 280 or more Turkish ships of the line, most of them galleys, supported by approximately 75 vessels of other types presented a fearsome sight to the heterogeneous group of Europeans from all parts of the continent.

The European fleet consisted of 212 galleys, 24 troop transports, and 6 galleasses—more or less. The numbers of vessels on both sides vary according to the source consulted; these seem to be the most reliable numbers.

The Ottoman line of battle, a thousand meters longer than that of their adversaries, completely blocked the entrance to the Gulf of Lepanto early on this first Sunday in October 1571. Over the waves, the allies could hear weird music as the Turkish sailors and soldiers danced about their decks to the accompaniment of tambour, cymbal, and flute. The Turks believed that they would that day either send the Christians to hell or themselves to heaven—hopefully both. The Ottoman admiral, Ali the Muezzin, observed that the League fleet was approaching in unusual formation. Ali was called "the Muezzin" because, as one of the few adult males they heard, he had achieved eminence by means of the effect his voice had on the women of the sultan's harem.

Going contrary to the usual procedure in the naval warfare of the time, Ali ordered his wings to fall back while his flagship at the center of the line brought the ninety-six galleys under his personal command to the fore. At the foremast of Ali's flagship, named *Sultana* in honor of the sultan's daughter who was his patron, flew the great green banner of Mecca.

Believed to be a replica of the flag carried by the Prophet, the ensign was embroidered in gold thread 28,900 times with the name of Allah. It was considered one of the treasures of Islam.

When the flag was carried by Ottoman troops into battle, they had never been defeated. Ali Pasha, to give the Turkish admiral his title, had also brought along some extra insurance for the battle: a sacred talisman, a tooth of the Prophet mounted in a crystal sphere.

Meanwhile, the League commander-in-chief, Don Juan of Austria (illegitimate but acknowledged half-brother of King Philip II of Spain), was exhorting his men. In spirit, though not in belief, his words were similar to the speeches of the imams who promised eternal bliss to the Turkish soldiers and sailors.

Iron crucifix in hand, Don Juan was rowed out to the ships under his direct command. He reminded each one in turn that he had done what he could and it was now up to them. They were to humble the pride of the Turks and gain glory. Whether they lived or died, they would conquer, for dying they would be welcomed in heaven.

From the Ottoman ships came hoots, catcalls, the sound of musical instruments, random shots . . . anything and everything to supplement their already intimidating and overwhelming presence. From the League fleet—by direct order of Don Juan—came nary a sound. Gradually this began to fray the nerves of the Turks, more accustomed to shouts of defiance or pleas for mercy than this ominous silence.

As if on cue, the wind, until that moment directly behind the Ottoman fleet, shifted almost 180 degrees to the west. The Turkish vessels slowed almost immediately, while the League galleys picked up speed and, with lateen sails billowing, bore down on the enemy.

Don Juan ordered the huge banner of the Holy League broken out from the mast of his flagship, the *Real* ("Royal"). A tremendous cheer arose from the entire League fleet, echoing across the water. The flag, personally blessed by the pope, bore the image of Christ Crucified. On signal from the *Real*, a crucifix was raised on every League ship.

For his part, Selim the Drunk had given Ali Pasha explicit orders to sweep the seas clear of all Western presence. Satisfied his imperial command would be carried out to the letter, he then went back to his liquor and his women.

To carry out the sultan's orders, Ali had gathered every available ship from throughout the Ottoman Empire. He manned them with the cream of the Turkish army and navy. Opposing the former muezzin was a League fleet composed of many disparate elements. The allies consisted of Catholic and Protestant, Christian and Jew, and a variety of nationalities that were ordinarily at each other's throats. There were even a few Muslims, Ottoman rule not being universally popular. The Turks expected internal dissension alone would win the battle for the forces of the Prophet.

The evident solidarity achieved by the League fleet should have given Ali pause, to say nothing of other factors. There was, for example, the unusual battle formation and the six huge Venetian galleasses. Each was armed with forty-four guns and had been towed into place a mile in advance of the rest of the fleet a short time earlier.

These vessels, actually floating gun platforms, had been positioned in pairs to anchor the center of the League line. They were a critical element of the battle plan. Around them, the fleet advanced, keeping almost to the letter of the battle plan worked out by old paralyzed Don García de Toledo, viceroy of Sicily during the siege of Malta, back in Spain.

There was thus serious cause for doubt in the Turkish ranks. Far from breaking up as the Turks expected, the League allies actually appeared to be coming together as a unified fighting force.

There was good reason for this show of unity. The "Holy League" that sponsored the fleet was the brainchild of Pope Saint Pius V. Pius was a stern and rigorous former inquisitor general who wore himself out in a few short

years as supreme pontiff. He was to die a few months after
Lepanto.

Unlovable though he might be to some modern eyes,
Pius V was the right man in the right place at the right time.
Nothing less than the discipline and order he imposed on
the Papal States and, by extension, on the rest of the otherwise ephemeral Holy League could have stood against the
frightening menace of the Turk.

The West, weak and tottering after the chaos of the Great
Schism, the strife precipitated by the Reformation, and the
conflicts engendered by the rise of nationalism, needed
someone to provide a rallying point and re-instill its faith
in itself. That someone was Pius V.

Immediately upon his election to the papacy, Pius set to
work with a determination as resolute as that of Selim II was
vacillating. To restore the West's will to resist required, in
the pope's view, a moral reformation.

In consequence, the former inquisitor general unhesitat-
ingly and vigorously encouraged works of charity and piety
among the people, setting the example himself. With equal
vigor, he pursued the immoral, the disruptive, and the criminal, sought to root out various forms of corruption among
the clergy, expelled those he regarded as subversive elements—such as Jews and Gypsies—from the Papal States,
and forced the reform of prostitutes, gamblers, idlers, and
the lazy.

Some of the pope's measures were less successful. Anxious to restore unity to Christendom, he, imprudently it
could be argued, threatened Elizabeth I in an attempt to
bring England back into the fold.

Although the Virgin Queen was generally under the thumb of her advisors and at the mercy of court factions and favorites, there was only so far anyone could push a member of the notoriously headstrong if weak-willed Tudor dynasty. Elizabeth failed to react as anticipated. Pius responded with an excommunication as disastrous as it was ineffectual. That said, the purpose of an excommunication, it should be remembered, is as much medicinal as it is disciplinary or punitive; it is to call the individual back to communion with the Church by making plain to them and others that they stand outside it.

Perhaps Pius could or should have been more politic, but it seems not to have been in his character. Saints are not often politicians, and politicians are almost never saints. Elizabeth, in turn, increased the persecution of Catholics in her realm. In another indication of his non-politic nature, Pius similarly alienated many Catholic rulers by his insistence on the separation of Church and State.

Nevertheless, the pope managed to hammer together an alliance to fight the Turks. Even Elizabeth sent men and money—the danger was that great. The pope ordered Masses celebrated and prayers offered without cessation in Rome.

At Pius's insistence, every Christian in the League fleet—Protestant and Catholic alike—went to confession, assisted at Mass, and prayed the Rosary right before the battle. In addition to strict gunnery drills, everyone fasted for a period before the battle, training their spirits as well as their bodies and minds for the unequal task to come. Jack Beeching, in his book *The Galleys at Lepanto*, credits this unity of religious practice, temporary though it was, with building morale and forging otherwise disparate groups into an effective fighting force.

There was only one possible choice as commander for such an endeavor. That was, of course, the incredibly popular Don Juan of Austria, the natural son of Holy Roman Emperor Charles V and a barmaid.

The charisma surrounding Don Juan is substantial even after the passage of centuries. His elder half-brother, Philip II of Spain, a more estimable figure in some respects who had everything but popularity and good health, still comes off a distant second.

It is to his credit that Philip did not let his obvious jealousy of his younger and far more popular semi-sibling overcome his good sense or his affection—too much, anyway. A lesser man would never have recognized Don Juan in the first place, or would have had him conveniently removed, possibly exiled to the New World where he would likely have died of fever as so many did in the early days of the Spanish seaborne empire.

In spite of his inexperience, Don Juan made some brilliant decisions (based largely on the advice of de Toledo)—and managed to enforce them in the face of the rather stodgy collection of advisors and admirals with which he had been saddled. The most fatal for the Turks was to unship the heavy rams or *esplones* that decorated the prow of each ship.

Some sources maintain that the rams were taken down on the advice of Gianandrea Doria, others that of de Toledo. Still others credit Don Juan himself with the idea.

What matters is that rams had been a feature of naval warfare in the Mediterranean for two thousand years. Their removal meant that the League fleet could not use the traditional tactics of ramming and boarding. They would have to rely on cannon and hand-to-hand fighting after coming alongside an opposing vessel or being rammed by an enemy ship. It also meant that each galley in the Holy League's fleet was materially more maneuverable than the Turkish vessels.

A decision that multiplied available manpower many times over in the League fleet was to unchain and arm the non-Muslim galley slaves. Criminal, debtor, Jew, or pervert, all were promised freedom if the League won the day.

Unlike some similar promises throughout history, this one would be kept. The slaves aboard the Turkish vessels—Christian and Jew—were forced below their benches and threatened with death if they raised their heads.

Ali Pasha at least had the decency to inform the slaves on his ship that Allah would free them either from their chains or life if he lost the battle. He had always treated his slaves better than most Turks.

The galley slaves of the Turks were there almost by choice. Since no Muslim could keep another Muslim as slave, all it required to be free was to recite the *inshallah*, the formula that makes one a Muslim. Most Turkish masters felt that those who refused to do this merited any treatment they chose to inflict.

As the fleets approached each other, Don Juan prepared another surprise for the enemy. Again contrary to accepted practice, which dictated that commanders stay as far to the rear as possible to direct matters properly and that flagships did not engage, the *Real* and the *Sultana* were seen moving toward each other as if to participate in a pre-arranged duel.

Formally opening the battle, Don Juan caused the first shot to be fired on the League side by discharging one of his bow cannons at ridiculous range as a challenge to Ali. He then ordered his sailing master to bring the *Real* alongside the *Sultana*. Before the two flagships could close, however, other vessels engaged.

To the right of the *Real* was the papal flagship commanded by Marcantonio Colonna. To the left was the squadron under the command of the Venetian Sebastian Veniero, an experienced sea-fighter considered a little cantankerous at times. He had earlier remarked to one of his officers that it would be a good day to die.

Veniero had been a friend of Marcantonio Bragadino, the Venetian senator who had been the civil governor of Famagusta on Cyprus so viciously tortured to death by the Turks after surrender and guarantees of safety. The men in the fleet of the Holy League had only the day before learned of the fate of their fellows in the Famagusta garrison.

Thinking that the clumsy galleasses in the League fleet would prove easy marks, the Turks rowed into close quarters. Very quickly they learned to their cost that long-range gunpowder and shot were more effective than close order rams.

When the Turkish vessels tried to close on the galleasses, volleys of harquebus fire tore through the massed boarding parties gathered on the decks of the attacking ships, while solid shot from cannon splintered the hulls of the vessels.

The Turkish line began to falter. Nevertheless, in the words of another naval hero centuries later, the men of the Holy League had not yet begun to fight.

The majority of the League gunners were still holding their fire. They had been advised not to shoot until they could make out the faces of the Turks.

When the order was finally given, the opening volley brought the Turkish line to a virtual standstill. The training and discipline drummed into the League soldiers and sailors paid off, especially in contrast to the laxity which overconfidence had instilled in the Ottoman host. Every shot fired by a Turkish vessel was met with three from a League ship.

The wisdom of eliminating the weight of the rams on the League vessels now began to pay off. The League ships rode high in the water. The Turkish gunners overcompensated, and shots from their galleys tended to be high and miss their mark, sailing harmlessly over the heads of their opponents.

Beveling fire from the League ships, however, was angled to allow for the fact that the enemy was riding lower in the water. Shots not only hit their mark but a large proportion managed to hit below the waterline, fatal in any naval battle.

The two flagships were now close to engagement. The figure of Don Juan in his gold-plated armor could be seen calmly strolling about the deck. His natural exuberance at last overcoming the calm religious demeanor he had been cultivating so assiduously, the bastard prince performed a brief galliard, capering wildly about the deck. Don Juan was famous for his dancing, and it must have been a sight to see.

Soon the ram of the *Sultana* crunched into the hull of the *Real*. Grappling lines were quickly attached and the two ships brought together to form a floating field of battle.

Harquebus fire and flights of arrows—those of the Turks were poisoned—raked the decks of both ships while grenades flew through the air. The Turks pressed forward to capitalize on the advantage they had gained by ramming the *Real*.

Unfortunately, the Turkish boarding parties, waiting so eagerly to swarm aboard the League flagship, met with yet another innovation: boarding nets. They were unable to carry the fight to the deck of the *Real*.

The Turks thereby had the disadvantage at sea of fighting on their own ground, the exact opposite of the usual situation in a land battle. The *Real's* boarding parties were not slow to press home their own advantage and gain the deck of the enemy ship.

Some say that the first to gain the deck of the *Sultana* was a woman, María la Bailadora, "the Dancer." She had allegedly sneaked aboard in disguise to be with her lover.

While some authorities may be generally opposed to the idea of women in combat, in this instance, it was singularly appropriate, even poetically just. The Turks had always specially targeted women and children as prey on campaign, regarding them as just one more variety of loot and subjecting them to slavery and every other imaginable degradation.

La Bailadora took revenge for generations of women and children. She is not only said to have boarded the deck first, she is also credited with killing her first opponent with a single thrust of her sword. After the battle, she was officially entered on the rolls of the regiment and given a pension.

The fight near the northern shore of the Gulf of Lepanto, the left wing of the League fleet, was fully as dramatic as that taking place in the center around the two flagships. The Ottoman right wing, commanded by Mehmet Scirocco (Mohammed the Wind), outnumbered the opposing Venetian galleys that made up the bulk of the League left wing.

The galley under the command of Marcantonio Quirini, a captain who had managed to run the blockade of Famagusta in January, was particularly hard-pressed. He was at the extreme end of the line of battle, and the goal of Mehmet Scirocco was to flank the League line.

Quirini was the anchor of the entire northern part of the battle and, thus, the chief target of the Turkish onslaught. Despite Quirini's efforts, the Turks did indeed manage to turn the flank, but were blocked in completing the maneuver by the rest of the Venetian contingent.

This spurred the Turks on to greater ferocity. The galley of Venetian admiral Agostino Barbarigo was targeted by a squadron of eight Turkish galleys, detached especially to take him out.

The order was given on the assumption that the loss of the Venetian leader would demoralize the rest of the contingent. This would give the Turks an open path to come up behind the League line.

They very nearly succeeded. Barbarigo was wounded in the eye by one of the Turkish poisoned arrows. He turned over command to his second, Federigo Nani, and retired from the fight, to die soon afterwards.

Loss of their admiral did not, however, have any apparent effect on the Venetians. For the past twenty-four hours, every single one of them had known of the fate of the defenders of Famagusta and how the Turks had broken their pledged word. The fight was a matter of personal honor for each Venetian, more than anxious to exact full payment in Turkish blood for the horrors perpetrated on Cyprus.

Still, the outcome of the fight hung in the balance, although perhaps leaning slightly in favor of the Turks. Six Venetian galleys had already been sunk, and a number of the Turkish vessels, pounded by cannonades from the floating gun platforms provided by the galleasses as well as the League galleys, were beginning to founder. The situation, viewed either from the deck of Don Juan's flagship or from the Ottoman perspective, was desperate.

HISTORICAL NOTE: THE GALLEY IN WARFARE

Some commentators have declared that both sides in the conflict used outdated military technology. The attitude seems to be that the galley, king of the Mediterranean for two thousand years, was obsolete in 1571.

Unfortunately, someone forgot to tell the naval powers that contested supremacy of the "Roman Sea." They continued to use the galley until the nineteenth century, when steam power finally made it possible for a warship to move at the requisite speeds for combat without relying on human muscle.

Myths about the galley abound. Most common, of course, is the role of the galley slave. Where would the novel *Ben Hur* (by General Lew Wallace, Indiana native, Civil War veteran, and New Mexico territorial governor, official nemesis of Billy the Kid) be without Judah ben Hur's bold defiance of the roman consul? And the consul's response: "We keep you alive to serve this ship. . . . Row well and live, Forty-one."

The fact is that "the galley slave" as depicted in countless works of fiction and films was unknown until the Renaissance. It was only then that the device was invented that permitted unskilled convicts, slave labor, and conscripts to row a galley, rather than the highly trained and well-paid professionals who propelled warships from classical times through the medieval period.

Ancient Rome acquired a navy by finding a beached Carthaginian galley and taking it apart to see how it was put together. They then frantically trained legionnaires to take their places at the benches by practicing on stools set up on the beach.

The galleys themselves were manufactured on an early assembly line using interchangeable parts two millennia before Eli Whitney reinvented the process. (There is evidence suggesting that the Romans dotted their world with prefabricated temples as well.)

The galley was supremely well adapted to warfare in the enclosed waters of the Mediterranean. It was able to maneuver quickly in a battle situation when there might be no wind, or the wind was from the wrong quarter.

That is the reason the galley held its own for so long, not any inherent resistance to change on the part of the surrounding naval powers. A military power that refuses to innovate soon finds itself defeated or conquered, as was the case eventually with the Ottoman Empire.

For centuries, the Turks insisted on using the tactics that had served them so well in conquering the Byzantine Empire and finally taking Constantinople in 1453. Those same tactics, however, virtually ensured defeat when the military technology and tactics of the West caught up and finally surpassed those of the East.

The fact is that wind has always been unpredictable as motive power. Motive power is, however, almost the only thing that matters in warfare, aside from weaponry—victory generally goes to whoever gets there "firstest with the mostest." Steam guaranteed the fall of the galley's eminence, not an obsolescence based on the rise of wind as motive power—however splendid a picture is presented by a tall ship under full sail.

The reason warships in the Atlantic and Pacific relied on sail instead of oarsmen is that a human engine is only feasible for short hauls and fast battles—such as characterized warfare in the Mediterranean. It would have taken far more food and water than a ship could carry to maintain even brutalized galley slaves in any shape to row a ship on a short ocean cruise. A warship needs to move fast, and it needs to have its motive power as far removed from the vagaries of nature as possible, but the power source also has to be alive when human muscle is doing the work.

Just as the galley was supremely suited to warfare in the Mediterranean, then, it was supremely unsuited to warfare in the open sea. When the Spanish Armada set out in 1588, there was an attempt to duplicate the success of the galleasses at Lepanto a few years before by using a number of the cumbersome ships. The wreck of one of these, the *Girona*, was discovered about forty or so years ago off the west coast of Ireland.

The Spanish apparently did not realize that galleasses' very cumbersome stability, an asset in Mediterranean warfare, was a distinct liability in the high seas of the Atlantic.

It simply could not be maneuvered with any degree of success. Examination of the wreck of the *Girona* suggests that it had been driven on the rocks out of sheer inability of the exhausted oarsmen to propel the ship out of danger.

There was more than one distinct advantage to the galley's passing, however. Aside from the utter filth that inevitably accompanied chaining slaves in place without rest or relief (when the wind was in the right—or wrong—quarter, the smell announced the approach of a galley long before it hove into view), replacing human slaves with the "energy slave" of steam meant that the market for slaves north of Africa began to dry up.

Of course, slave raiders found new markets in sub-Saharan Africa and continue down to the present day to ply their age-old trade.

11

LEPANTO II

1571

DESCRIPTIONS of the battle of Lepanto usually make the progress of the struggle sound very orderly, and the proceedings almost stately. This is supported by the many—the very many—paintings and engravings that depict the battle.

There is also the testimony of a poet who was insulted more than forty years after the battle by a literary critic. The critic sneered at the writer for wounds received at Lepanto, as if that somehow affected the quality of his work. To this the poet replied,

> What I cannot but resent is the fact that he describes me as being old and one-handed, as if it were in my power to make time stand still for me, or as if I had lost my hand in some tavern instead of upon the greatest occasion that the past or present has ever known or the future may ever hope to see. If my wounds are not resplendent in the eyes of the chance beholder, they are at least highly thought of by those who know where they were received. The soldier who lies dead in battle has a more impressive mien than the one who by flight attains his liberty. So strongly do I feel about this that even if it were possible to work a miracle in my case, I still would rather have taken part in that prodigious battle than be today free of my wounds without having been there.

The poet being mocked, of course, was Miguel de Cervantes Saavedra, and the piece of literature being ridiculed was *El Ingenioso Hidalgo Don Quixote de La Mancha.* Despite the honor and glory of having taken part in the battle, however, an objective observer would probably have concluded that the struggle resembled little more than a confused mess. Of course, the same could be said of almost any battle in history. It is a well-known military aphorism that no battle plan ever survives contact with the enemy. That should be kept in mind in examining the rest of the battle.

Nor was future knowledge available to those engaged at Lepanto. Accounts today make it sound as if it could only have ended in victory, but the real case was far otherwise. Up until almost the last moment it could have gone either way. It was, as the Iron Duke of Wellington would say of another pivotal battle at Waterloo, a near run thing. . . .

OUR LADY OF VICTORY

The struggle on the right wing of the Christian fleet during the long day of October 7, 1571, in the Gulf of Lepanto was in sharp contrast to the frenzy that characterized the fighting on the left wing and in the center. The action on the right bore a closer resemblance to a carefully planned game of chess, although one marked by impetuous gambits and long chances by everyone except the League admiral.

Under the direction of the venerable Gianandrea Doria, the fleet maneuvered carefully against his old antagonist, the Christian renegade El Louck Ali, Turkish governor of Algiers. He is better known to history generally by the westernized version of his Islamic name, "Ochiali."

Both Doria and El Louck Ali had been less than enthusiastic about the fight. Each had tried to persuade his respective commander to put it off to another day.

Still, while the opposing squadrons maneuvered to gain a more favorable position, individuals and groups took heroic measures. Alessandro Farnese, Duke of Parma, personally led his followers off the Genoese flagship on to the nearest Turkish galley. He charged with such force that the enemy vessel was captured almost completely intact.

In another part of the battle, a young poet by the name of Miguel de Cervantes was put in command of a longboat. The idea was to create a diversion by rowing to the opposite side of an enemy ship that had been grappled, boarding it, and attacking from the rear.

Cervantes apparently accomplished his mission. He was wounded at least twice, in the breast and the left hand, "to the greater glory of my right," as he put it later.

Two factors handicapped Doria. One, half the galleys under his command represented a private investment. Risking them might mean losing them, and thus his capital. Two, El Louck Ali had met Doria twice before and had defeated him on both occasions.

Nevertheless, Doria apparently managed to convince himself that this time he could defeat the wily pirate by outmaneuvering him. This meant refusing to close with the enemy. Doria received a sarcastic, if rather gentle, reprimand during the review after the battle when Don Juan remarked in passing on the undamaged condition of the Genoese admiral's flagship.

In a duplicate of what was happening on the left wing of the Christian fleet, El Louck Ali attempted to flank the Genoese galleys and get inshore of them. Both Doria and El Louck Ali began to extend their lines, El Louck Ali to carry out the flanking maneuver, Doria to prevent it. Don Juan, observing what was happening, sent a message to Doria to break off the maneuver and bring his vessels back into line. El Louck Ali's forces outnumbered Doria and could easily carry out a movement that had baffled Mehmet Scirocco on the left wing.

Doria ignored the order. Instead, he began to move his galleys toward the southern shore of the Gulf of Corinth, the other name for Lepanto.

What Doria apparently did not realize (but which Don Juan had seen instantly) was that his attempt to halt El Louck Ali's flanking maneuver opened up a sizable hole in the League line of battle. Once this was large enough, the renegade immediately gave the order to put over the helm and drove his ships through the hole before neighboring League galleys could fill the gap.

El Louck Ali's flanking attempt had been a feint. A sizable number of Turkish galleys poured through, and the day could have been lost right there.

The renegade, however, had a strong instinct for self-preservation. He may have divined from what he observed in the center of the battle the way it might go—to his personal cost.

Demonstrating more cunning than patriotism, El Louck Ali abandoned the slower vessels in his command. Instead of coming up behind the line of the Holy League, which would have been disastrous for the League fleet, he made a run for home.

Had El Louck Ali flanked the League fleet, he would very likely have forced the center of the battle to shift away from the fight in progress between the two flagships, the *Real* and the *Sultana*. As it was, however, it was becoming clear that the duel between the two commanders could very well decide the outcome.

Possibly as many as eight hundred combatants on both sides were engaged in a vicious back and forth struggle on the main deck of the Turkish flagship. Twice, the League soldiers fought the Turks almost to the stern of the *Sultana*, whence the Turks rallied both times and pushed the *élite* contingent from the *Real* into the bow.

The *Real* herself was riddled with Turkish arrows, deadly to man, but incapable of inflicting any real damage to the critical fallback position provided by the intact hull of the League flagship. Seven Turkish galleys stood in reserve to the *Sultana*, constantly supplying fresh troops. As Ali Pasha's men fell, they were immediately replaced from these reserves. The men from the *Real* had no such reinforcements.

Don Juan received a wound in the leg. He shrugged it aside, both then and later.

In spite of the animosity traditionally reported by historians between Don Juan and his half-brother, Philip II, there seems to have been genuine affection between them. Don Juan did not want to burden Philip with worry over his physical condition. It was bad enough that the younger man's gallantries and chivalric gestures were a constant source of exasperation to the more staid king of Spain.

There was no need for Don Juan to bother Philip with a wound that only resulted from having put himself in danger that his brother would have regarded as unnecessary.

The men of the *Real* made a third rush against the Turks, this time pressing the Ottoman force all the way to the poop deck in the stern. At this point, a harquebus bullet struck Ali Pasha in the forehead, killing him instantly.

One of the armed Christian galley slaves leaped forward and hacked off the Turkish admiral's head. He hurried to present it to Don Juan but was ordered to throw it into the sea after the young commander viewed the grisly trophy with distaste.

Another sailor rescued it, stuck it on a pike, and hoisted it up in full view of the opposing forces. With the heart taken out of the Turks on their flagship, the *Sultana* was soon in the hands of the League.

The green flag of the Prophet was hauled down and quickly replaced with the banner of the Papal States. A trumpet blast drew attention to the action.

In the hold of the *Sultana*, the soldiers and sailors found an immense treasure—150,000 gold zechinni, or sequins. These were coins equal in value to an imperial gold ducat or two silver thalers (dollars).

Ali, fearful that the sultan's possible displeasure could result in a confiscation of his wealth, had brought everything he owned to sea with him. Ironically, his enemies became his *de facto* heirs.

In spite of the loss of the *Sultana*, the Turks were not yet defeated. The battle raged on in the center and on both wings.

Sixteen of the galleys El Louck Ali abandoned in his flight were now engaged with eight League galleys under the command of Don Juan de Cardona. The fighting was so vicious that every man aboard two of the papal galleys died either in the battle itself or afterward of wounds received. Of the five hundred Sicilian soldiers aboard de Cardona's ship, a bare 10 percent survived unwounded.

Observing the struggle and with his own fight over, Don Juan of Austria came to the rescue. Seeing his approach, some of the Turkish captains beached their galleys rather than continue the fight and ran away, thinking that possible death on land was better than certain slavery at sea. The commander-in-chief's timely arrival broke the back of what remained of a Turkish force that could have turned the tide of battle had El Louck Ali led them into the fight instead of saving his own skin.

The fighting, however, continued.

Although he was seventy-five years old, Sebastian Veniero, stationed to the left of Don Juan's *Real*, took an active part in the battle. He insisted on firing the first shot from his ship with a harquebus, point blank into the faces of the bow gunners of the Turkish galley bearing down on him.

After that, Veniero contented himself with a crossbow, a weapon with which he was more familiar. Too feeble to crank the windlass himself, a sailor was detailed to assist him.

Veniero could still discharge his weapon, however, and calmly concentrated his bolts on the Turkish sharpshooters who had been assigned to bring him down as opposing admiral. Picking them off one by one, he exclaimed that he would count himself fortunate if his days should end in such a battle, God willing.

On the left wing, the Turks under Mehmet Scirocco were beginning to press home their marginal advantage. With a ferocity born of desperation, having just lost Ali, his commander-in-chief, Scirocco might well have been able finally to complete the flanking movement he had been attempting from the beginning.

At a critical moment, however, the galley slaves in Scirocco's contingent broke free of their chains and threw themselves into the battle. Working in secret, they had filed through their iron manacles.

At a prearranged signal from the leaders of the conspiracy, they rose and attacked the Turks from the rear. They spread chaos through the Turkish forces by clubbing their erstwhile masters with broken lengths of chain or strangling them with bare hands.

Mehmet Scirocco was killed in the hand-to-hand fighting, probably one of the first targets of the newly freed galley slaves. His body was found floating face down in the sea, recognizable only by the elaborate robes customarily worn by high-ranking Ottoman officials. The Venetians hauled his corpse from the water, chopped off its head, and raised it aloft in grim imitation of what they had just seen on the *Real*.

A somewhat ironic, if slightly humorous, note can be inserted into the account of the Venetian part of the battle. The galley slaves in the Venetian vessels, in compliance with Don Juan's orders, had been armed and promised freedom in return for their cooperation and assistance in the fight.

The Venetians, however, were notorious for finding ways out of deals that cost them money, and Venice, with its sea empire to maintain, was perennially short of galley slaves. Now that the tide of battle was beginning to ebb, an enormous crowd of debtors, Jews, heretics, perverts, and thieves launched themselves over the sides of the galleys to wade ashore and begin a new life in the mountains of Albania, most of them as bandits.

Clearly the battle was nearly over. On the right wing, El Louck Ali began looking around for some easy target to silence criticism and impress the sultan. He needed something to divert attention away from the fact that he had saved himself and some of his ships only at the cost of losing the battle.

The renegade found what seemed to be a suitable prize to assuage any imperial ill feelings on the part of the sultan. This consisted of three galleys under the command of the Knights of Malta. The Knights were objects of especial hatred to Selim and, perhaps more importantly, to his harem.

The Knights had been responsible for the disastrous outcome of an investment by the harem in the expedition on Malta six years before. Valette, the capital of Malta, is named in honor of the Grand Master during the siege, Jean Parisot de la Valette.

In addition, the Knights had been plundering shipping deep in Ottoman territory for years, their crusading spirit still undimmed. They were a constant thorn in the flesh of the sultan, hurting his pocketbook as well as his pride.

El Louck Ali took seven of his galleys and headed straight for *La Capitana*, the Knights' flagship under the command of their prior Pietro Giustiniani, a personal enemy of the renegade. El Louck Ali cut out *La Capitana* and grappled all seven of his vessels alongside.

It cost the renegade over three hundred of his men to take down the thirty Knights and their supporting men-at-arms, but he succeeded. He left only Pietro Giustiniani and two other Knights (who appeared to be dead) alive. Giustiniani had been felled with five arrow wounds and was to all appearances the only survivor of the unequal struggle—and that only because the renegade needed him as a hostage. The rest of the Knights' squadron fought equally well.

El Louck Ali now had what he had come for, a prize and a prisoner. He hauled down the great ensign of the Knights and secured his trophy.

His personal mission accomplished, El Louck Ali turned and started to make good his escape. Unfortunately for him, however, he was spied by the rearguard under the command of Don Alvaro de Bazan, the Marqués de Santa Cruz.

This was a force of thirty galleys kept in reserve with orders to intervene only where necessary. The battle nearly over, they felt free to pursue the renegade before he could make his getaway.

Now the goal was not to win the battle. That had already been accomplished.

Efforts now were directed to ensuring that not a single Turk of rank escaped. With every other Ottoman admiral dead, El Louck Ali was the only one of any significance left. The fact that he was considered a traitor caused even the galley slaves to set to work with a will to capture him or, at least, relieve him of his prize.

One galley managed to pull ahead in the race to capture El Louck Ali, *El Guzman* under the command of Captain

Ojeda. He managed to bring his ship alongside *La Capitana* and board her.

With his finely-honed instinct for self-preservation, however, El Louck Ali cut loose *La Capitana*. Abandoning the prize crew he had put aboard the captured vessel, he made for the open sea. As a reward for his heroic act of rescue, the Knights gave Captain Ojeda a life pension.

El Louck Ali, in command of a bare fourteen galleys and galliots, was the only effective naval force the Turks had left in the entire Mediterranean. Still, he needed some insurance before he dared appear before Selim.

He cruised about for a few days until he came across a straggler returning from the battle, a Venetian galley. He captured it and immediately made his way to Istanbul, hopefully secure in his position as the only survivor of any importance.

Sokolli, the Ottoman grand vizier, relieved El Louck Ali of his trophy and had the Knight's ensign from *La Capitana* displayed in the mosque converted from what had once been the Hagia Sophia, the Church of the Divine Wisdom, the principal shrine of Orthodox Christianity. It is doubtful that anyone was fooled into thinking that it was a memento of a great victory.

Enraged, Sultan Selim ordered the massacre of every Christian slave in Istanbul. As with many of his drunken ravings, his advisors ignored the order. His successor, Murad III, would order the death of every Jew in the empire, only to be dissuaded by a gigantic bribe . . . which was probably what he was after in the first place.

Losses in the fleet of the Holy League are estimated between 7,500 and 8,000 men, with the Venetians being hardest hit. Turkish losses are harder to gauge. Estimates range from a low of 25,000 to a high of 60,000.

Part of this is due to the fact that few Turkish vessels survived. Counts were made primarily on the basis of the number of turbans found floating in the water and collected as trophies.

It is certain, however, that Turkish losses were enormous. There was scarcely a family throughout the empire that did not sustain some loss.

Appropriately enough, the galley *Angelo Gabriele*, named in honor of the herald archangel, brought the news of the victory to Venice in a bare ten days, sailing into the lagoons with a huge Turkish flag and a long line of turbans dragging in the water. At first, seeing sailors in turbans, the citizenry thought it was an Ottoman advance scout.

They were quickly reassured when the crew began firing off the guns and shouting, "Victory! Victory!" Reception of the news was even more enthusiastically received due to the fact that it was only the day before the city had received news of the atrocities perpetrated at Famagusta.

Credible witnesses reported that Pope Pius V, like Moses, remained kneeling in prayer on the day of the battle. At approximately four o'clock in the afternoon—when the battle was definitely over—the pope suddenly rose and ordered that a *Te Deum*, a hymn of thanksgiving, be sung in all the Churches of Rome.

Pius flung open a window and declared to his treasurer, who had come to recite the usual litany of papal financial woes, "Go with God. This is not the time for business, but to give thanks to Jesus Christ, for our fleet has just conquered." Official word only reached Rome by way of

Venice two weeks later . . . and yet the pope knew some-how that his prayers had been answered.

Celebrations rivaled those of Mafeking Night centuries in the future—or perhaps it should be said that the jubilation of Mafeking Night, when news reached London on May 18, 1900, that the town had been relieved after a 217-day siege, was a pale imitation of the near-hysterical relief over the victory at Lepanto. Even pickpockets and whores took the night off. The euphoria was echoed throughout Europe. Elizabeth I ordered a special prayer of thanksgiving read at all services throughout England.

Some historians credit the rebirth of the Baroque style of architecture to the elation that followed the battle and the need to immortalize the victory in every possible way. These included a pulpit shaped like a galley prow in Irsee in Bavaria, a stained glass window at Wettingen in Switzerland, and, of course, captured flags and trophies everywhere.

The great artists of the day competed to see who could turn out the most splendid depiction of the battle. Tintoretto painted a huge canvas, which established his reputation. Andrea Vicentino painted one bigger, and put himself in the picture. Outdoing them both, Veronese created a vast allegory that was placed directly above the doge's throne in Venice.

A new altar was consecrated in the church of San Guiseppe, a new entrance put on the famous Arsenal of Venice, and a new charitable confraternity created exclusively to celebrate October 7 each year as the Feast of Our Lady of Victory. This was the *Scuola del Rosario*, emphasizing the role played by having everyone in the Christian fleet pray the Rosary before the battle.

Still, the victory was not all it could have been. The Holy League lacked the internal coherence to hold together except in the face of the enemy. With the immediate threat eliminated, the League dissolved. The alliance was unable to follow up on what was described by many contemporaries as a miracle.

Turkish power, though not eliminated as a threat, would henceforth be in decline at sea. It would be another half century before the tide began to turn on land.

HISTORICAL NOTE: CROWN OF ROSES

As a result of the battle of Lepanto, the Church proclaimed October 7 as a day of perpetual remembrance as the Feast of Our Lady of Victory. This was later changed to the Feast of the Most Holy Rosary, as many people credited the recital of the mysteries of the Rosary, "Mary's Crown of Roses," with gaining divine assistance for the League.

The entire month of October was henceforth officially dedicated to this devotion. Even many Protestants made a point of reciting the decades of the Rosary in thanksgiving for a period after the battle. It is not unheard of down to the present day to find various Protestants on an individual basis who find this private devotion of great spiritual benefit.

The Rosary did not originate in 1571, however salutary its benefits were found to be at the time. Catholics generally credit Saint Dominic, the founder of the Dominican

Order (the "Order of Preachers" or OP) with instituting the Rosary. Current research suggests that Saint Dominic likely formalized a practice that had already achieved some currency and popularized it, so it would be correct to acknowledge him as the "father" of what we know as the Rosary.

Recitation of the Rosary has been credited with overcoming a number of political and military threats, even in modern times. Under the title of Our Lady of Prompt Succor, the nuns of the Ursuline convent in New Orleans, in company with the wives, sisters, and daughters of the soldiers under General Andrew Jackson guarding the city in 1814, petitioned the Blessed Virgin through the Rosary for her intercession on behalf of their loved ones.

Jackson himself credited the astonishing victory to the fervent prayers of the Catholic sisters. Immediately after the battle, he sent one of his officers to thank the nuns, showing up the next day with his entire staff to thank them in person. The tiny statuette venerated by the nuns still exists and is ensconced today in a rebuilt convent.

US Marines in the Pacific theater in World War II found on occasion that after the Japanese had been driven off of an island, the native peoples were terrified of the American military. The Japanese had filled their heads with tales of cannibalism and torture allegedly perpetrated by these strange-looking, pale-skinned, round-eyed, foreign devils. They assured the islanders that these weird creatures would treat the natives like wild animals, not stopping until they had exterminated them as vermin.

Once, after occupying an island, the Marines tried to give food and water to natives obviously starving to death

but were refused with looks of deep suspicion. They had been told that the Americans would offer them poisoned food and drink and preferred starvation to the effects of an unknown drug. Nothing assuaged their fears, not even graphic demonstrations in which Marines would eat some of the proffered food themselves. (The Americans were immune or had taken the antidote, of course.)

Finally, one of the Marines noticed a religious medal hanging around the neck of one of the islanders. On a sudden impulse, he took out the Rosary he carried with him and displayed it to the group of natives. Problem solved. The natives ate and drank without fear.

Many Austrians claim that the nationwide Rosary Crusade after the Second World War kept the country out of the hands of the Communists and its almost certain subsequent absorption into the Soviet Empire. A German Jesuit in Hiroshima credited the fact that he was the only person near ground zero to survive the dropping of the bomb to his daily recitation of the Rosary.

Does the Rosary really have these effects? All Christians believe God hears our prayers and sometimes answers them in miraculous ways, most especially when two or more are gathered in His name. So, to the believing Christians of the day, the mass of prayers offered up for that great victory at Lepanto would certainly have been viewed as playing a significant role in the events at sea. Many continue to believe so today.

It is true that such belief is not exactly something conducive to scientific verification. What is beyond question, however, is the fact that morale can make a difference in overcoming odds that seem insurmountable. Without a doubt, something inspired the soldiers and sailors of the Holy League to set aside their differences, deep and divisive as they were, and come together as a cohesive fighting force that enabled them to overcome the mightiest and most fearsome empire on earth.

12

KHOTIN

1621

LEPANTO did not end the Ottoman threat. For the peoples of eastern Europe from the sixteenth to the nineteenth centuries, the Grand Turk was more than a pantomime figure or a phantasm to frighten children. He was a very real and palpable menace that had conquered large portions of the region and raided the remainder continually for slaves and loot.

For the Ottoman Empire, eastern Europe constituted a vast training ground for their "unconquerable" armies, as well as a reservoir of wealth, especially slaves, to be plundered at will. We may disagree completely with Marx's and Engels's prescription for social betterment, but we have no quarrel with Engels's analysis that declared Ottoman imperialism a threat to all European development, whether socialist, capitalist, or any third alternative.

Not that Europe accepted this situation lying down. Even after the enslavement of the Balkan Peninsula and, with the help of the Tartar Crimean khan, the northern coast of the Black Sea, resistance to Ottoman aggression was strong and continual.

The Rus, Don Cossacks, Zaporozhie Cossacks, and Moldavians all managed to interfere to some degree with the

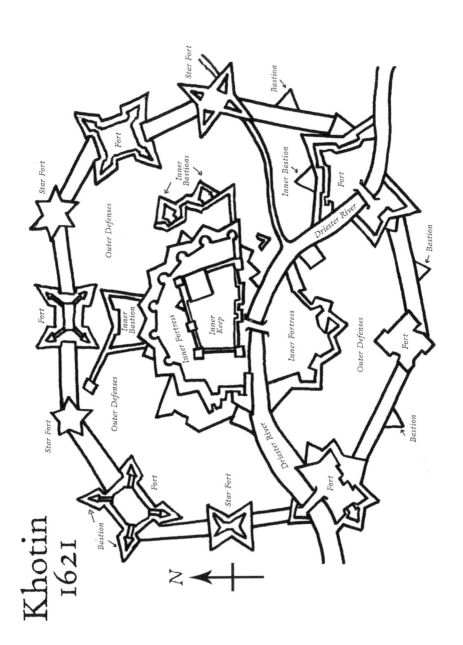

Khotin
1621

N

Star Fort

Bastion

Inner Bastion

Driester River

Fort

Bastion

Fort

Star Fort

Inner Bastions

Outer Defenses

Inner Bastion

Inner Fortress

Inner Keep

Inner Fortress

Outer Defenses

Fort

Fort

Outer Defenses

Star Fort

Fort

Bastion

Bastion

Star Fort

Driester River

Fort

plan of the Grand Turk—the Ottoman sultan—for world conquest. Ironically, it was probably to poke the Turks in the eye and prevent a rumored Ottoman campaign into *Mitteleuropa* that provided a pretext for yet another attempt to open up the road to Vienna.

From the tail end of the sixteenth century to the beginning of the seventeenth, the Polish-Lithuanian Commonwealth began intervening in Moldavia, a Turkish vassal since the days of Mehmet II, "the Conqueror." Nor did it help any that the Cossacks, technically governed by the Commonwealth, tended to view Ottoman territory as their legitimate field for raiding.

The Poles had managed to stay out of the Thirty Years' War that was then tearing the Holy Roman Empire apart. King Sigismund III Vasa of Poland did, however, send the *Lisowczycy*, an *élite* mercenary regiment, to his Habsburg allies.

In 1619, the *Lisowczycy* engaged and defeated the forces of George Rákóczi, a nobleman of Transylvania, at the battle of Humenné. Prince Gabriel Bethlen, ruler of Transylvania, then appealed for help from the new, eighteen-year-old Ottoman sultan, Osman II.

Anxious to prove his mettle, wanting revenge against the Commonwealth, and with a corps of extremely restless janissaries to placate, Osman readily agreed. He assembled a large army and sent it north under the command of Oczakov Iskender Pasha.

For once, there was a near-legitimate pretext for the invasion. The Polish chancellor, Stanisław Żółkiewski, had led a small force into Moldavia in September of 1620. This was ostensibly in support of the local Turkish overlord, Gratsian, whom the sultan had ordered removed from office.

The Poles and various allied Cossack groups engaged in some minor pillaging and cattle stealing. They accomplished nothing of importance, other than to provide a pretext for a Turkish counterstrike.

The raiding party under Chancellor Żółkiewski was annihilated at the battle of Cecora on September 20, 1620. The Turks followed up with Tartar raids into southern Poland.

On October 7, 1620, the strategically vital fortress of Khotin was stormed and taken. Significantly, the capture occurred on the forty-ninth anniversary of Lepanto.

The Turks, however, abandoned the fortress and withdrew their forces. The area was not subject to Islam, which for the Turks meant their sultan. It would have been dangerous to leave such an exposed salient deep in enemy territory, even in a position so strongly fortified.

As the onset of winter was near, the campaign was suspended. The ease with which Żółkiewski's raiding party had been destroyed and Khotin taken, however, convinced Osman of the weakness of his adversary. He decided that the time was ripe to conquer the great Polish-Lithuanian Commonwealth and, in the spring, renewed the war with the army under his personal command. . . .

BEGINNING OF THE END

It was more than a little reminiscent of the stand at Thermopylae nearly two thousand years before. A band of 200 Zaporozhie Cossacks stood with their backs to the Pruth

River. They faced a Turkish force composed of as many as 150,000 battle-hardened veterans.

Another one hundred or so Cossacks had taken up positions on the other side of the river. Members of the first group had engaged themselves to buy enough time for their comrades to gain the fortress of Khotin in safety. They retreated to a series of caves that lined the bluffs along the river and awaited the arrival of the armies of the Grand Turk—Sultan Osman II—that had left Istanbul April 29, 1621.

Osman had recently come to the throne at age eighteen as a result of the janissaries deposing another recently ascended sultan a few months previously. The new sultan had to prove himself to the janissaries in order to secure his throne—and his life.

The slave soldiers of the Ottoman Empire demanded action and needed it in order to gain loot, fame, prestige, even heaven. And that, a restive janissary corps, as even the great Süleymân the Magnificent had discovered, could be a problem.

Consequently, the sultan caused the horsetail standard to be paraded through the streets of Istanbul and the call to battle cried throughout the Ottoman Empire. As soon as he had enough men and material assembled, he left Istanbul at the head of his army. On the march, he collected units from his European territories, Walachia and Moldavia. The Crimean khan, Dzhanibeg Gerei, also joined his forces with those of the sultan.

Osman had collected a force that was estimated at between 120,000 and 150,000 battle-hardened veterans, along with ordnance consisting of sixty-two cannon.

Turkish cannon were, at this time, technologically superior to those of the West.

While things appeared desperate, however, matters were not as bad as they seemed. Osman had made a serious mistake and badly misjudged the political and military situation.

For all its inherent weaknesses—structurally, politically, and militarily—the Polish-Lithuanian *res publica* remained a significant power. "The Deluge" that began with the Cossack Rebellion of 1648 that shattered the great union was still nearly a generation in the future.

In the face of the Turkish invasion, the Poles fortified Lvov, Kracow, Kamenetz, and other strongpoints. Overall command of the Polish forces, estimated at roughly thirty-three thousand men supported with twenty-eight cannon, was given to the Grand Duke of Lithuania, Yakub Karl Khodkyevich. Khodkyevich had gained renown as the victor over the Swedes at Kircholm in 1605 in a stunning display of the effectiveness of Polish-Lithuanian *hussaria*, eastern Europe's famed heavy cavalry.

Still, outnumbered both in men and equipment, the Polish-Lithuanian Commonwealth had no choice but to seek allies. Sigismund III Vasa, king of Poland, appealed to the Orthodox patriarch of Jerusalem, Feofan, for assistance.

The patriarch was at that time traveling from Moscow to Palestine. En route, he received the Polish request that he persuade the Zaporozhie Cossacks of the Ukraine, followers of Orthodox Christianity, to attack their common enemy.

Feofan realized that, for all the differences between the Latin and Greek Churches, the real enemy was the Turk.

Feofan's appeal on behalf of Poland and Lithuania mobilized the Cossacks and Ukrainians. The *rada* (a sort of Cossack *posse comitatus*) gathered on June 15 in Sukho Dubrav, between Rzhishchev and Beloe Tserkov.

The newly elected chief, or "hetman," of the Cossacks, Jacob Nerodich Borodavka, selected between thirty and forty thousand well-armed and experienced troops to send against the Turks. Although primarily light cavalry, and extraordinarily effective as such, the Cossacks also brought twenty-three cannon. This brought the allied forces to an estimated sixty-five thousand, lowering the estimated odds facing the allies from five-to-one to two-to-one.

Borodavka had risen to eminence from the Cossack lower classes. He had been elected hetman of the Zaporozhie Cossacks near the end of 1619 with much popular support. He replaced the incumbent, Hetman Sagaidichi, who was given a lesser, but still important, command, being sent north to Warsaw to serve as liaison to the Poles for the coming conflict.

By the middle of August, the Zaporozhie Cossacks under Hetman Borodavka had crossed the Dneister River into Moldavia. The Polish detachments, approaching the Dneister from the north, began to cross to the fortress and town of Khotin. In order to do this, however, they were forced to construct a bridge across the river, which had apparently reached flood stage.

Khotin (with seemingly numberless variant spellings) was a fortified town in what is now Ukraine. The old fortress is in the southeast quarter of the town, which is in the Chrnovitskaya Raion (region). It is located at 48 degrees 30 minutes north and 26 degrees 30 minutes east. It is situated on the right bank of the Dneister, near the Romanian border, a little south of Kaminetz.

In the Middle Ages, the Genoese had a colony and stronghold at Khotin to facilitate trade with Crimea and the Black Sea coast. The population a century ago was 18,126. At that time, there were local industries making leather, candles, beer, shoes, and bricks, but in medieval times, the town was important primarily as a military outpost defending the trade route along the Dneister. The location was of critical importance, both militarily and commercially.

While interesting, however, and important to understand the significance of the siege of Khotin, this information did little for the Cossacks facing the first onslaught of the Ottoman forces.

The Cossacks had been assigned the role of vanguard, over the protests of Hetman Borodavka. This was in accordance with Sigismund's master plan for the battle.

Borodavka's compliance with the Polish-Lithuanian demands earned him several rebukes from his countrymen, dissatisfied with what seemed to be their new chief's subservience to the foreigners. With some justification, they saw Cossacks being sacrificed for Polish and Lithuanian interests.

Sigismund, however, was hoping that the well-known Cossack ferocity would serve to blunt the force of the Turkish offensive. This would gain time for the Polish-Lithuanian forces, many of which were late in arriving, to gather at Khotin.

The detachment led by Prince Wladislav (later Wladislav IV of Poland) was delayed longer than most. Wladislav's force only reached Khotin on September 1, crossing the river the next day.

Unlike many military commanders through the ages (granting the truth of the adage that "no battle plan survives contact with the enemy"), Borodavka managed to carry out his assignment. He preserved the majority of his forces and concentrated them near the Dneister in the region of Molgilev. From there, he sent various Cossack detachments in different directions to scout and locate the enemy while, at the same time, providing a cavalry screen to confuse the Turkish advance. Some detachments went as far as Jassy and Suchavi, where they skirmished briefly with the forces of the sultan. It seems likely that Borodavka also sent a body of six thousand Cossacks directly to Khotin at this time, possibly with the thought of using them as a reserve.

Ukrainians hold the actions of the detachment that raided Suchavi high among their national heroic exploits. Still, despite their courage and audacity, the Turks drove the Zaporozhie back to Molgilev.

What happened next is obscured by a great deal of confusion and available reports in English that are as sketchy as they are contradictory. Piecing together the evidence and making certain educated guesses from what happened later, events seem to have unfolded as follows.

The Zaporozhie Cossacks under Hetman Borodavka were forced together with other Cossack units near the Pruth. As noted, Borodavka probably sent six thousand of his men to Khotin and, with the remaining force of twenty-five to thirty-five thousand, prepared to halt an Ottoman army at least four times its size.

The subsequent action near the banks of the Pruth is credited with being the opening of the battle of Khotin. Badly outnumbered, many of the Zaporozhie Cossacks were killed.

A significant number were taken prisoner; again, available records in English are more than a little sparse on specifics. Some sources are not even clear whether there was a first engagement or how it developed. What is clear is that while the balance of the Cossack force under Borodavka managed to withdraw in relatively good order, the Turks remained in possession of the field.

To gain time for his retreat and to allow the remnants of the main force to reach Khotin, Borodavka left a tiny rear guard consisting of no more than three hundred survivors of the first action. Of these, approximately two hundred somewhat optimistically concealed themselves in ambush in the woods that lined the right bank of the Pruth. Another one hundred or so occupied a series of caves along the left bank near the road that constituted the only approach to Khotin for the sultan's army. After this, the story becomes much more clear.

On August 18, the Turkish column appeared on the road. As soon as the enemy was within range, the Cossacks opened fire.

The Turks were as much surprised by the audacity of the attack as by the fewness of their adversaries, whom they assumed had already been annihilated. The Turkish advance halted—but not for long. Their first response was to attempt to brush aside what seemed to be a minor nuisance and continue the march.

The Zaporozhie Cossacks, however, refused to accommodate themselves to the wishes of the enemy. Continued resistance resulted in the decision to burn them out of the caves. The Turks managed to set the material in the caves alight, which forced the defenders from their refuge. Half-blinded with smoke, coughing, and confused, the Cossacks charged from the caves, shooting arrows at random. Fighting only ceased when all the Zaporozhie on the left bank had been slain.

The Turks were still faced with the problem of crossing the Pruth in the face of the *sotin* ("hundred") of Cossacks hidden on the opposite side of the river. At first, Sultan Osman directed his janissaries to lay an artillery barrage into the woods.

Whether from an inability to direct fire accurately against the concealed opponents or from the difficulty of penetrating the thickets with the ordnance at the command of the Turks, the attack was unsuccessful. The Zaporozhie were able to beat back all assaults and prevent a Turkish crossing of the river.

When night fell, the Cossacks abandoned their fortifications, having done all they could to hold up the Turkish advance. Not more than thirty of them were taken prisoner during the withdrawal.

One seventeenth-century Ukrainian chronicler, not without reason, compared the exploits of the Zaporozhie Cossacks on the banks of the Pruth to Leonidas and his Spartans at Thermopylae. They had inflicted enormous losses on the Turkish army and held up the advance on Khotin for a full twenty-four hours. This gave the main Cossack body the opportunity to elude the enemy and unite with the Polish and Lithuanian forces a bare day before the Turks arrived at the re-occupied fortress of Khotin on September 2.

Hetman Sagaidichi had arrived at Khotin from Warsaw on August 21, anxious that all credit for any victory not go to his political rival. He assumed command of the six thousand Cossacks who, arriving before him, had been sent to the main Polish-Lithuanian force by Borodavka, although exactly when is not clear.

Some historians have asserted that Sagaidichi was in command of the six thousand from the beginning. An eyewitness contradicted this. Jan Sobieski, whose grandson was to win fame as the victor at the second battle of Khotin more than half a century later and, especially, for his relief of Vienna in 1683, was in command of a Polish detachment at Khotin. He noted in a dispatch that Hetman Sagaidichi joined the forces at Khotin after the Cossacks detached by Borodavka had already arrived.

The main body of the Zaporozhie arrived at Khotin on September 1. While the allied force was nowhere near as numerous as the opposing Turkish army, it was still too large to fit inside the castle.

A fortified camp was laid out surrounding the fortress in a well-defended location. The weakest point of the defenses was from the west, which was the only way that admitted easy access to the camp. It was anticipated that the Turkish army would concentrate its efforts there.

Consequently, the defenders constructed two high stockades directly across the most obvious route for the Turkish assault. A number of strongpoints were built in front of this double wall to protect the approaches. A wide moat was dug between the double wall, while the ground was cleared in front of the fortifications for a distance of about two hundred meters.

The Zaporozhie Cossacks took up a position south of the Poles and Lithuanians, outside the main camp. This was on a flood plain of the Dneister.

Initially the Cossack defenses consisted solely of drawing up a double line of carts. These were quickly improved upon when trenches were dug to provide cover from enemy fire.

A critical advantage gained by the sacrifice of the Cossacks on the banks of the Pruth was that there was time to lay out the defenses in such a manner that the artillery, consisting of twenty-eight Polish and twenty-three Cossack cannon, was able to cover all approaches to the camp.

Against this the Turks had a minimum of sixty-two guns, most of them of much larger caliber than those of the allies. On the other hand, the allies had a slight edge in small arms and infantry. Most of the Turkish force consisted of light cavalry, usually no match for either European-style formed infantry or the Polish-Lithuanian *hussaria*.

The Polish infantry, under the command of Prince Stanislas Lubomirski, took up a position on the right flank. The center of the line, commanded by Prince Wladislav, was filled by late arrivals such as recently hired foreign mercenaries, mostly German and Swiss *Landsknechten*, and miscellaneous other detachments.

The Lithuanians and Belorussians held the left flank under the command of Lithuanian Grand Duke Jan Karol Khodkyevich. He was old and seriously ill but still well able to plan an effective campaign. In the gap between the Lithuanians and the Zaporozhie Cossacks were more detachments of *hussaria*. The river anchored the Zaporozhie line.

Probably counting on exhaustion from the earlier fight at the river, the Turkish vanguard attacked the Zaporozhie Cossacks on September 2. They were driven off toward evening thanks to the timely arrival of Lithuanian cavalry detached by Khodkyevich from the left flank, some German *ritteren* (knights) from the center of the line, and the nearby Polish *hussaria*.

The allied war effort appeared to be operating at maximum efficiency, much like a well-oiled machine. This mutual support among the allies is given a great deal of credit for the eventual victory. After this initial repulse, the Turks retired to await the arrival of the main force.

Two days later, early on September 4, the main body of the Turkish army arrived. Almost immediately, in an attempt to take the allied camp by storm, the assault began. Although the fighting continued throughout the day, the effort was of no avail.

The Turks then decided to change tactics and instituted a systematic siege. A detachment of *sipahis* was sent across the Dneister to cut communications between Khotin and Kamenetz, the Polish supply base. At the same time, detachments of the Crimean khan's forces began ravaging the country around Lvov and Zamostya, probably in an attempt to draw the allies out from behind their fortifications.

It was not until September 7 that the Turks once again attempted to storm the camp. Probably on the advice of either spies or deserters, they concentrated on attacking two of Prince Wladislav's infantry companies that were composed of raw recruits.

Fortunately, Grand Duke Khodkyevich's reserves were sent to their relief almost immediately and succeeded in driving back the assault. The Lithuanians drove the Turks from the wall and began a limited pursuit. Turkish losses for this effort were estimated at over 1,500 men, among them Mustapha Pasha, bey of Baghdad.

As a result of his enormous losses in infantry, Osman decided to order four thousand janissaries from his personal guard to attack the Cossacks. This attack, too, was beaten back.

The sultan raged and stormed. This campaign, begun a few months after his coronation, was initiated to prove that he, not yet twenty years of age, was destined to play the role of another Süleymân the Magnificent or Mehmet the Conqueror. Events were clearly not turning out as planned.

Only reinforcements supplied by Karakasha Pasha, bey of Buda (the capital of Hungary under Turkish control), now gave Osman any hope of success. Karakasha Pasha, at the head of five thousand janissaries and twenty-one thousand *sipahis*, attacked the allied camp on September 15. He concentrated on a section of the Polish right flank, which, according to a deserter, was weakly defended.

The attempt almost met Sultan Osman's expectations. Scaling the walls, the Turks penetrated deep into the camp.

Khodkyevich, however, quickly organized a counterattack by the foreign infantry, largely composed of the efficient and ferocious *Landsknechten*. Karakasha Pasha was killed in the attack, and the Turks fled, panic-stricken. The Zaporozhie Cossacks took the opportunity to harry the fleeing Turks from the rear and slew more than three hundred of them.

Osman, for some reason, blamed his grand vizier, Hussein Pasha, for the failed attack and replaced him with Dilaver Pasha. These frequent changes in command structure and tactics seriously weakened the morale and effectiveness of the Ottoman host.

On September 24, Grand Duke Khodkyevich died, worn out by what could only be described as superhuman efforts for a man of his age and condition. Other, less reliable, reports have the grand duke dying on the last day of the siege.

Learning of his death, the Turks decided that his Lithuanians would refuse to take orders from Prince Lubomirski, the Polish commander. The basis for this belief, in light of the splendid cooperation they had already seen among the allies, is somewhat obscure.

In any event, early on September 25, the Turks began shelling the camp from the south and west, as well as from across the Dneister. A massed attack on the camp was launched at noon.

Although the outcome of previous attacks gave no real indication that the attack might be successful, the situation of the allies was indeed grave. The lines of defense had been shortened due to heavy losses, the allies having been forced to withdraw from some of the outlying fortifications.

The Turks still seriously outnumbered the defenders, both in men and ordnance. They took as much advantage of this as they were able and managed to seize control of the allied center, ensconcing themselves in the defenses formerly held by the foreign mercenaries and the Zaporozhie

Cossacks. From here they launched a series of attacks against the now-open position of the Polish-Lithuanian *hussaria*. Prince Lubomirski, however, counterattacked almost immediately. He charged the Turks on their right flank, where they were engaged with the *hussaria*.

The Turkish position now became as deadly to the Turks as it was perilous to the allies, for it put them in range of two masked cannon. Gunners raked the open ground with crossfire.

This caused hundreds of casualties among the Turks before they had to cease fire when the Cossacks threw themselves into the thick of the fighting. The Cossacks intermingled with the ranks of the attackers and put them to flight. Once again the Turkish assault was driven off.

The next day, September 26, the Turks renewed shelling the Cossack position from across the Dneister, where they had eighteen cannon. Apparently the range was a little too extreme, however, for they were unable to inflict much damage. Aware of the difficult situation of the besieged, Osman attempted to tighten the blockade further.

Two days later, Osman decided to make one final push to destroy the allied forces. On September 28, he ordered all his forces concentrated for one final assault.

A skeleton force of ten thousand janissaries of the sultan's personal guard were left in camp as reserves. Batteries totaling forty cannon were positioned across the river, whence fire was directed against the positions of the Cossacks and Poles.

The forces of the Crimean khan, along with a number of *sipahis* and janissaries, were also concentrated across the river in an attempt to divert the Polish-Lithuanian *hussaria* from the main attack. In this, they do not appear to have been successful.

The first Turkish assault was directed against the Polish-Lithuanian *hussaria*, located on the left flank, which ground they held between the Lithuanian infantry and the Zaporozhie Cossacks. The idea was probably to try and eliminate the single most effective, and therefore dangerous, threat in the allied ranks.

Consistent with their tradition as the Commonwealth's shock troops, the *hussaria* charged forward in advance of the main body of allied troops. They were successful in driving off eight attacks.

Under the force of the assault, however, some of the defenders began to fall back from the walls. The line was stiffened by reinforcements sent by Prince Lubomirski as well the Zaporozhie Cossacks who were attempting to regain their former position in the defenses. By themselves, the Zaporozhie drove off a total of eleven attacks.

Having failed to eliminate the threat posed by the *hussaria*, the Turks finally decided to attack the weak center of the allied line as the day drew to a close. There, however, sudden volleys from two concealed cannon stopped them in their tracks. These were possibly the same two guns that had wreaked such havoc on the previous occasion.

Losing their momentum, the Turks became sitting ducks for the Polish artillery. This was particularly effective because of the confusion in the Turkish ranks. The guns were loaded with a chilling combination of lumps of iron and shards of glass. This lethal mix cut great swaths through the Turkish ranks.

The assault ended in complete failure. A Turkish chronicler attempted to explain away the disaster by asserting that the janissaries had acted weakly and ineffectively, and that this was the reason for Osman's later decision to attempt to disband them. This decision cost Osman his life—the first instance of the regicide of an Ottoman sultan.

The allied losses, relatively speaking, were not great. Failure of the final assault forced Osman and his new grand vizier to negotiate a settlement.

Although the request was made on September 29, the negotiations did not start until October 2, with the allied contingent headed by Jan Sobieski. As a bargaining chip, the grand vizier demanded on behalf of the sultan that the Commonwealth recognize its dependence on the Turkish empire, send an annual tribute, and suppress the Cossacks. Quite possibly the only realistic gain the vizier hoped to attain was the elimination of Cossack raids into Turkish territory.

Naturally the allies, in the person of the Polish delegation, refused to submit to the Turks and become vassals of the sultan. In view of the battle that they had just fought to a draw, the demand was patently ridiculous. They also refused to pay tribute, a demand clearly made to have something over which to dicker.

On the most important demand that they suppress the Cossacks, the Poles made a counter-demand that the Turks stop the Tartar raids. To better their own position, the allies then demanded compensation for losses suffered in the battle.

At this point in the negotiations, the vizier shifted from threats and demands for tribute to pleading for the Cossack raids to stop—the real issue. On dependence or paying tribute, nothing more was said.

The vizier agreed to settle for a one-time "gift"—a bribe—to the sultan in exchange for an agreement to withdraw Turkish troops beyond the frontier. The first battle of Khotin was over.

The vizier's anxiety to settle quickly was probably aggravated by reports that a large contingent of Don Cossacks was nearing Khotin. These had been summoned by Borodavka during the *rada* held on June 15, but had delayed the start of the expedition until after the return of a large number of their fighting men who were away at sea.

It was not until September 29, however, that the vizier received word from Kamenetz that twenty thousand Cossacks were approaching, certainly enough to turn a drawn battle into a rout. It is not clear whether the vizier made the request for negotiations before or after receipt of the report. The news that such a large body of reinforcements was approaching, however, certainly made a settlement more critical for the Turks—as well as explaining why Sobieski delayed three days before commencing talks.

The first battle of Khotin is a noteworthy example of the military cooperation of Russian, Ukrainian, Belorussian, and Lithuanian peoples with the Poles. As at the battle of Tannenberg in 1410 against the invading Teutonic Knights, a feared and powerful enemy faced them. The Turks threatened the independence and the very existence of the Ukrainian, Polish, and Lithuanian peoples and sought to perpetuate the subjugation of the southern Slavs.

News of the victory quickly spread throughout Europe. While officially a draw, it was clear that only circumstances

KHOTIN   257

had prevented a complete Turkish defeat, as the sultan's troops seemed to realize. The Turks had begun their decline in sea power at Lepanto. Khotin marked the beginning of their long decline in Europe. Serious—and nearly successful—efforts to conquer Europe would continue, but the menace of the Grand Turk was beginning to fade.

Fading, yes, but the threat was far from over . . . as later events would prove. In 1657, for example, Transylvania, the eastern portion of the former Kingdom of Hungary that had been a semi-autonomous part of the Ottoman Empire, attacked the Tatars and their allies, the Turks. By 1662, the war ended in defeat for the Hungarians, and both western and eastern Hungary came under direct Turkish rule.

The Turks attacked Austria in 1663 but were defeated at the battle of Saint Gotthard, August 1, 1664. Retaining the city of Nové Zámky in what is now southwestern Slovakia, the campaign marked the limit of Ottoman expansion in Hungary.

Due to the refusal of the Sejm, the legislature of the Polish-Lithuanian Commonwealth, to grant funds to Jan III Sobieski (1629–96), the Polish-Ottoman War of 1672–76 ended in a draw. The Turks gained two-thirds of Ukraine but lost future tribute from the Poles.

The Great Turkish War of 1683–99 began when the Turks assembled an invasion force of 150,000 to attack Vienna. Protestant Hungarian nobles rebelling against the Catholic Hapsburgs joined with the Ottomans.

Austria, the Polish-Lithuanian Commonwealth, Venice, and Russia joined together in a new Holy League as the Turks invested Vienna. In one of the greatest cavalry charges in history, Jan III Sobieski, at the head of the winged hussars, routed the Turkish forces, preventing a lengthy siege of Vienna. The Ottoman historian Silahdar Findiklili Mehmed Agha described the three-hour battle as the greatest defeat ever suffered by the Turks.

The Holy League re-conquered Hungary, and the Venetians attacked Greece and conquered the Peloponnese. At Zenta, in what is now Serbia, on September 11, 1697, the Hapsburg forces surprised the Ottoman army as it was crossing the Tisa River. Suffering only a few hundred casualties to the thousands lost by the Turks, the victory at Zenta eventually forced the Ottoman Empire to agree to the Treaty of Karlowitz in 1699, by which they lost most of their possessions in central Europe.

But all of these just mentioned above may constitute a future volume, perhaps titled *Ten More Battles Every Catholic Should Know.*

HISTORICAL NOTE: THE WINGED HORSEMEN

What were the *hussaria*? The first impulse is to equate them with the light cavalry regiments employed by European armies in the eighteenth and nineteenth centuries—the hussars. That, however, gives the wrong impression.

The western European troopers were certainly inspired by the Polish original but were a radically different type of soldier, filling a completely different role. There is no exact equivalent in English for *hussarius*. The best that can be done is a description rather than a name.

The word *hussar* is derived from the southern Slavic for "horseman." In central Europe during the fourteenth century, it denoted a mounted knight. As the Ottoman

Empire expanded deeper into south central Europe in the fourteenth and fifteenth centuries, many refugees from the Turkish menace found themselves in Hungary. At that time, the Magyar kingdom was still a strong bastion against Ottoman aggression. These refugees were welcomed because of their experience in fighting the Turk. Entire troops of these mounted soldiers were formed in Hungary. They were known collectively as hussars or *hussaria*.

Largely as a result of their contact with the then-advanced military arts of the East and the role played by the *sipahis*, or Turkish cavalry, contingents of *hussaria* fought as highly maneuverable and effective units on the battlefield. At the time, a typical cavalry battle involved a series of duels over which commanders exercised very little control once fighting began.

The idea of maneuvering as a unit rather than the lone chivalric hero was, for its time, truly revolutionary. Its like had not been seen since the glory days of the Late Roman Empire in the East and their famous *cataphracti*, the heavy cavalry that ably defended the Byzantine state—when permitted to do so by the bureaucracy.

The Polish-Lithuanian Commonwealth, despite its perennial quarrels with the Western Roman Empire and involvement in the seemingly eternal Guelph and Ghibelline conflict, had very close ties with Hungary. The first hussar regiments were formed in the Commonwealth to serve as light cavalry by the end of the fifteenth century.

After a few generations, these regiments evolved into heavily armored assault cavalry. This was a role unique in all of Europe.

Hussaria were sometimes referred to as "Polish Cossacks," at the time a complimentary, if not entirely accurate, label. "Cossack" seems to have been used on occasion as a synonym for cavalry. This makes researching the battles of the period somewhat confusing when trying to determine whether the "Cossacks" mentioned are Don, Zaporozhie, Poles, Magyars, or Lithuanians.

In spite of such trivialities, *hussaria* were the pride of the Polish-Lithuanian army until the end of the seventeenth century. That was when "the Deluge," which began with the Cossack Revolt of 1648, initiated the long process that brought about the effective end of Polish and Lithuanian autonomy until the twentieth century.

In response to several factors, the style of Polish-Lithuanian warfare evolved differently from that of western Europe. In the Holy Roman Empire and Italy, primarily because of the developments by the Swiss and German *Landsknechten* mercenary troops, infantry was becoming much more important than cavalry.

The situation was different in the Commonwealth. Until the seventeenth century, the Polish-Lithuanian *res publica* expanded rapidly. At its height, it encompassed nearly 1 million square kilometers, about 390,000 square miles. Distances were vast compared to other parts of Europe. Armies had to move quickly. In response to this need, cavalry became predominant.

Because of its strategic location, the Commonwealth served as a bridge between East and West. During the sixteenth and seventeenth centuries, it shared borders with Russia, Crimea (where the remnants of Genghis Khan's Tartars had settled), and the Ottoman Empire. Ottoman

Turkey included Greece, the Balkans, Romania, and Hungary. Included in the mix were the Holy Roman Empire and Sweden. Each of these neighbors used different military techniques, so the Commonwealth was forced to invent new tactics to counter them all—individually and collectively.

Young nobles formed the backbone of the *hussaria*. In the Commonwealth, every property owner, regardless of the size of his estate, qualified as "noble" and was technically eligible for election to the kingship.

In return for the elevated social and political position the gentry enjoyed, they had certain responsibilities. Besides acquiring an education, gentlemen were expected to spend a few years in the military.

They would later serve as reserves to be called up at need. Most young men were superb horsemen and experienced with arms long before serving in the army. They were first-class military material.

Cavalry constituted 80 percent of the Commonwealth's armed forces in most campaigns. *Hussaria* were heavy assault cavalry, whose main task was breaching enemy formations with charges at top speed. Given the vast distances involved, western European "hedgehog" formations were impracticable in central and eastern Europe, as their inability to maneuver meant they could easily be circumvented.

Because the gunpowder weapons of the time took much longer to reload than today, heavy cavalry was extremely effective in breaking through enemy lines. It was only necessary to wait until the enemy let loose a volley, then charge. Arms typically consisted of a lance along with horse pistols and heavy sabers.

"Wings"—steel frames decorated with feathers attached to the upper body armor—were characteristic of the *hussaria*. These appear to have been intended to absorb the force of the slash of an opponent's saber coming from behind or the side. They also were designed to overawe the opponent's horses and men. Other armor consisted of the more familiar helmet, breastplate, and protection for arms and legs, especially the knees, a vulnerable area for cavalry.

These "Winged Horsemen of the Steppes," while they may seem weird or fantastic to modern eyes, were an extremely mobile and devastatingly effective fighting force until the early eighteenth century. This was when improvements in personal firearms, such as the flintlock and rifled barrels, began to give infantry more mobility and greater offensive capability.

SELECT BIBLIOGRAPHY

Many sources overlap; these are general categories based loosely on the theaters of war.

BYZANTIUM AND THE CRUSADES

Friendly, Alfred. *The Dreadful Day: The Battle of Manzikert, 1071*. London: Hutchinson, 1981.

Froissart. *Chronicles*. London: Penguin Books, 1978.

Joinville and Villehardouin. *Chronicles of the Crusades*. New York: Dorset Press, 1985.

Nicolle, David. *Manzikert 1071: The Breaking of Byzantium*. Oxford: Osprey Publishing Group, 2013.

Norwich, John Julius. *Byzantium: The Apogee*. New York: Viking, 1991.

———. *Byzantium: The Early Centuries*. New York: Viking, 1988.

Obolensky, Dimitri. *The Byzantine Commonwealth: Eastern Europe 500-1453*. London: Phoenix Press, 1971.

Oldenbourg, Zoé. *The Crusades*. London: Phoenix Press, 1966.

Ostrogorsky, George. *History of the Byzantine State*. New Brunswick, NJ: Rutgers University Press, 1969.

Treadgold, Warren. *A History of the Byzantine State and Society*. Stanford, CA: Stanford University Press, 1997.

THE OTTOMANS

Babinger, Franz. *Mehmed the Conqueror and His Time*. Princeton, NJ: Princeton University Press, 1978.

Clot, Andre. *Suleiman the Magnificent*. London: Saqi Books, 2005.

Goodwin, Jason. *Lords of the Horizons: A History of the Ottoman Empire*. New York: Henry Holt and Company, 1998.

Kinross, Lord. *The Ottoman Centuries, the Rise and Fall of the Turkish Empire*. New York: Quill Books, 1977.

Lewis, Bernard. *The Muslim Discovery of Europe*. New York: W.W. Norton and Company, 2001.

Palmer, Alan. *The Decline and Fall of the Ottoman Empire*. London: John Murray Publishers, 1992.

Wheatcroft, Andrew. *The Ottomans*. New York: Viking, 1993.

THE MEDITERRANEAN AND SOUTHERN EUROPE

Beeching, Jack. *The Galleys at Lepanto*. New York: Charles Scribner's Sons, 1983.

Bradford, Ernle. *The Great Siege: Malta 1565*. London: Penguin, 1964.

————. *The Knights of the Order, St. John, Jerusalem, Rhodes, Malta*. New York: Dorset Press, 1972.

Brockman, Eric. *The Two Sieges of Rhodes: The Knights of St. John at War 1480-1522*. New York: Barnes and Noble Books, 1994.

Chamberlin, E. R. *Everyday Life in Renaissance Times*. New York: G. P. Putnam's Sons, 1967.

Hitchens, Christopher. *Hostage to History: Cyprus from the Ottomans to Kissinger*. New York: The Noonday Press, 1989.

Kyrris, Costas P. *History of Cyprus*. Nicosia, Cyprus: Nicocles Publishing House, 1985.

Lane, Frederic Chapin. *Venetian Ships and Shipbuilders of the Renaissance*. Baltimore, MD: The Johns Hopkins University Press, 1992.

Mariti, Giovanni. *Travels in the Island of Cyprus*. Cambridge, UK: Cambridge University Press, 1909.

Morris, Jan. *The Venetian Empire, A Sea Voyage*. New York: Harcourt Brace Jovanovich, 1980.

Norwich, John Julius. *A History of Venice*. New York: Alfred A. Knopf, 1982.

Seward, Desmond. *The Monks of War, the Military Religious Orders*. London: Penguin Books, 1995.

Walsh, William Thomas. *Philip II*. Rockford, IL: TAN Books and Publishers, 1987.

CENTRAL AND EASTERN EUROPE

Castellan, Georges. *History of the Balkans: From Mohammed the Conqueror to Stalin.* New York: Columbia University Press, 1992.

Fregosi, Paul. *Jihad in the West: Muslim Conquests from the 7th to the 21st Centuries.* New York: Prometheus Books, 1998.

Hanák, Péter, ed. *One Thousand Years: A Concise History of Hungary.* Budapest: Corvina, 1988.

Lázár, István. *Hungary: A Brief History.* Budapest: Çorvina, 1997.

McNally, Raymond T. and Radu Florescu. *Dracula, Prince of Many Faces, His Life and His Times.* Boston: Little, Brown and Company, 1989.

————. *In Search of Dracula, A True History of Dracula and Vampire Legends.* New York: Warner Paperback Library, 1973.

Péter, Lázló. *Historians and the History of Transylvania.* New York: Columbia University Press, 1992.

Török, Béla. *Hungary and Europe: A Historical Review.* Sydney, AU: Hungaria Publishing Company, 1979.